This book, *A Life for God*, is a cor
Rabbi Greg Hershberg's series of m̲.........................ᵍⱼᵛⁱ ᵉᵗᵉᵣⁿⁱᵗy.
Those messages were met with such enthusiasm that we believed a
written form would also be valuable for believers. The following
endorsements are based on this book as well as those original messages.

For most Gentile Christian believers there is a huge disconnect
between the message of the Old and New Testaments. In *A Life
for God*, Rabbi Greg Hershberg masterfully weaves together both
messages, revealing their intended unity. God's ordained plan of
redemption, spiritual growth, and eternal life, foreshadowed in the
Old Testament, is unveiled in the New.

Dr. H. Dean Haun
Former President of the Tennessee Baptist Convention
Senior Pastor, First Baptist Church of Morristown, TN

After reading this book, I had a much clearer understanding and
appreciation for the incredible price paid for my salvation. Rabbi
Hershberg has done an amazing job of answering the most important
question in life – *what must I do to find eternal life and why does eternity
matter?* A treasure chest of wisdom, this book will enrich your life.

Jonathan Bernis
President and CEO, Jewish Voice Ministries International

This particular series helped us to not listen to the voice of the adversary. The Holy Spirit revealed to us the fact that He finds us very precious to Him – having us go through what we went through and how
we ought to see that sanctification process as an incredible honor.
It has helped us understand and love the Lord more. Sometimes the
thought and visual of living in eternity with Him overwhelms me
more than my earthly problems and makes me indescribably happy.
There is nothing like it, and I know this blessing of deepening my
relationship with Him, with all of its scary yet truthful aspects, are
preparing me for that glorious day.

Briana Lamberson
Delaware

The teaching on eternity caused me to cry as it touched the depth
of the soul when Rabbi Greg described the anguish Jesus felt on the
cross. It is a blessing beyond words to have Scripture come to life.
Rabbi's passion for the Lord is what makes his portrayal so profound.

Deborah McCormick
Macon, Georgia

Rabbi Greg Hershberg never fails to pour out on his listeners what God has poured into his heart and this is extremely evident in the *Living for Eternity* series. To go away from any of his teachings without a deeper understanding of God and encouragement to love, obey and worship Him more, would make me question if I had listened to a single word.

Benita Blake
Huntsville, Alabama

What I loved about his series *Living for Eternity* is that as believers in Yeshua, we can live with our feet permanently planted on earth while we prepare for eternity by focusing on God's kingdom agenda in the present. Lastly, he communicates clearly that the good news is all about Jesus and only through him we can find our hope and salvation.

Mrs. Donna Gutierrez
Dallas, Texas

I was moved to tears many times! And have shared this series with everyone I know.

Nora and Jack Burkhart
Texas Believers

I watch Rabbi Greg preach every Sabbath online. Hearing his sermons filled with his deep love for God has inspired me to search and seek within myself to believe God is truly the one and only God. God will always provide the tools we need to serve him if we just have faith that He is real and will keep His promises. I feel so much closer to God in these last ten months after studying the Scriptures with Rabbi Greg. He brings the love of God alive and real to us.

Jean Wise
New Smyrna Beach, Florida

These messages include descriptions of some of the symbolism seen in the Bible. For example, Rabbi touched on the Scripture in Psalm 22:6 where it talks about the "Worm." To the casual observer, this deeper dive into a seemingly insignificant word had such profound meaning. It could have been an insect. But no, it was a worm. A worm that is all flesh. And flesh is sinful. If I had to pick just one thing to say about these messages, it's how much I have learned that every single word in the Bible is significant.

Allison Terry
Fishers, Indiana

Living for Eternity taught by Rabbi Greg causes us to take note that we are truly pilgrims passing through this life. Our faith is seen in action and how we as believers conduct our lives. We do not live for the temporary, because our goal is to live for eternity with true riches to bring to our one true God the glory that is due His Holy Name.

Linda Wright
Fort Valley, GA

Rabbi Greg has been blessed by the Lord with a refreshingly unmistakable and wonderfully accurate interpretation for Scripture. Within moments of talking with him or listening to him teach God's Word, you know without a doubt that he has been gifted by the Father to deliver His message to a lost and dying world. I dare say it truly is "Scripture being taught the way it was intended to be" – like Yeshua (Jesus) taught.

Lance Pilgrim
Macon, GA.

Rabbi Greg's direct and no nonsense approach along with his N.Y. humor captivated me. The Hebrew and Greek translations with cross references in this series (as in all his teachings) helped me better understand God as my Father. I have never felt as close to God in all my years of church going as I do now. I have a clearer understanding of the world and my role in it. Consequently, I have changed my priorities.

Barbara Magowan
Clearwater, FL

The thing that stood out to me most about this series is that as a believer, my life becomes the best evidence of God's love and involvement with His people.

This life cannot produce that longing, and despite the hardships of striving through the narrow way, when God's promises are truly in focus, the longing just gets more intense.

This life vs. the life to come isn't even a contest.

David Beairsto
Bartonsville, PA

All of Rabbi Greg's sermons are anointed in my opinion, but *Living for Eternity* puts the believer's walk into a simple focus. He puts the walk of the Way into terms the simplest of believers can understand.

Philip (Tony) Beauchamp
Mocksville, North Carolina

Rabbi Hershberg goes deep into the Word and provides insights into the books of the Bible we might otherwise overlook or not fully understand. He provides details and imagery that are enriched by his Jewish heritage and that help us as Christians to know more fully what God's Word is really saying. Drawing correlations between God's number for grace (five) and the number of different sacrifices in Leviticus was an eye opener. His discourse on the types of wounds Christ suffered and what they represented was revealing, to say the least. I pray for all believers to hear and assimilate these and other truths and to become more fully committed to the true God, whom they will know more fully after hearing Rabbi Hershberg.

Shirley Smith
Hillsdale County, Michigan

In the Rabbi's series *Living for Eternity*, there are two areas in particular that weigh on me. In the third message, Rabbi is mentioning in Isaiah 53:10 about how it "pleased ADONAI to crush him," and in message four Rabbi is speaking about "unbroken fellowship with the Lord." I never in my whole walk have stopped to think about the Father, my Father Abba, until recently. These teachings have opened my heart in a way that is fresh with a new desire for God more than ever. They have greatly helped me understand the love our God has for us as Father. I truly thank God for Rabbi Hershberg, for the Jewish people, and their nation. Who would have thought, a central Florida redneck would end up studying like never before because of a Rabbi.

Shane Howell
Central Florida

Rabbi Greg is truly a man who loves God. His series on *Living for Eternity* is exactly how we as believers are to walk out our love for God. I thank God for using such a wonderful man who truly loves God and people. I cannot wait to listen to his message each week!

Donna Manley
River Hills, WI

Rabbi's teaching in this series has helped me to gain a deeper understanding of what true service is and how important it is to follow Yeshua's leading, especially in these turbulent times. I feel the call to share His grace and truth to everyone I meet, sometimes without saying a word.

Judith Sanders
Cochran, GA

Rabbi Greg, as always, breaks down the words of every study in the Hebrew and Greek. In this case, it was the Sh'ma. He broke down this wonderful command brilliantly, word by word. It gave us an understanding of God's Word that would have taken years for us to learn by ourselves.

Through Rabbi's teaching, we really "get" what God is saying, and it enriches us and blesses us deeply in our daily walk.

Pirtle Family (Ron, Jeannie, Rhonda)
Eugene, Oregon

The series of messages on *Living for Eternity* really helped me understand the sacrificial system of Leviticus. The L-rd truly blessed us with a rabbi to teach us and break down the Jewishness of the Scriptures. The comparison of the offerings to Yeshua the Messiah was so eye opening and so moving, it brought us to tears.

Lisa Vinson

Listening to the series *Living for Eternity* by Rabbi Greg has made my spirit come alive again. What Adonay Yeshua sacrificed for us is beyond human understanding. I pray everyone who reads this book will return to their "First Love" and glorify our Father in heaven Who loves us and sacrificed His only begotten Son so that we can be with Him for eternity.

Tamara Romines
Portland, Oregon

Rabbi Greg's messages are a blessing. His series *Living for Eternity*, has helped me as a Gentile to understand I am grafted in to Messiah through the Jews. I realize that one must understand the Jewishness to appreciate the heart and mind of God.

Brad White
Chesapeake, Virginia

As I listened to *Living for Eternity*, it was so refreshing and cut deep into my heart about the first and the most important Mitzvah of all. We say the commandment over and over, not knowing the true meaning of it. I appreciate the fact Rabbi Greg took time to explain the meanings in Hebrew root words. When we understand the original intention of the words, only then do we understand the true meaning.

Subashini Hirschler
Charlotte, NC

A LIFE
for
GOD

Listen to the original *Living for Eternity* messages: https://goo.gl/27okc2

A LIFE
for
GOD

A Rabbi's Analysis of Life,
the Cross, and Eternity

RABBI GREG HERSHBERG

We love hearing from our readers. Please contact us
at www.anekopress.com/questions-comments with
any questions, comments, or suggestions.

Visit Rabbi Greg's website: www.bethyeshuainternational.com
A Life for God – Rabbi Greg Hershberg
Copyright © 2017
First edition published 2017
All rights reserved.

Scriptures taken from the Complete Jewish Bible by David H. Stern. Copyright
© 1998. All rights reserved. Used by permission of Messianic Jewish Publishers,
6120 Day Long Lane, Clarksville, MD 21029. www.messianicjewish.net.
Cover Design: Natalia Hawthorne, BookCoverLabs.com
eBook Icon: Icons Vector/Shutterstock
Editors: Sheila Wilkinson, Heather Thomas, and Ruth Zetek

Printed in the United States of America
Aneko Press – *Our Readers Matter*™
www.anekopress.com
Aneko Press, Life Sentence Publishing, and our logos are trademarks of
Life Sentence Publishing, Inc.
203 E. Birch Street
P.O. Box 652
Abbotsford, WI 54405

RELIGION / Christian Life / Inspirational
Hardback ISBN: 978-1-62245-466-2
Paperback ISBN: 978-1-62245-462-4
eBook ISBN: 978-1-62245-463-1
10 9 8 7 6 5 4 3 2 1
Available where books are sold

Contents

Introduction

W hat comes to your mind when you think about eternal life? How does one live with eternity in mind, and what does a life for God look like? Do you imagine doing good deeds, kneeling for prayer, or singing in the choir? Do you picture almighty God sitting on a throne, weighing your good deeds against your bad? Just the phrase *a life for God* might sound religious and holy, but it doesn't give us direction as to how to accomplish it. If we think we want to live this way, we need to search for someone who can tell us how and not lead us down a path of error.

Do we turn to a hellfire-and-brimstone preacher who pounds on the pulpit and hopes to scare us into acceptance and submission? Isn't that what Jonathan Edwards did with his "Sinners in the Hands of an Angry God" sermon?[1] Edwards taught about the dangers of sin and the horrors of hell. He wanted people to understand the terror of being lost and facing the wrath of God.

The prophet Jonah may have preached a similar message as he walked through the streets of Nineveh. The city was so large it would have taken Jonah three days to cross it, but

---

1   Jonathan Edwards, "Sinners in the Hands of an Angry God," *Selected Sermons of Jonathan Edwards,* ed. H. Norman Gardiner (New York: The MacMillan Company, 1904), 78: *www.gutenberg.org/files/34632/34632-h/ 34632-h.htm.*

the people believed God after the very first day. *Now Ninveh* [Nineveh] *was such a large city that it took three days just to cross it. Yonah* [Jonah] *began his entry into the city and had finished only his first day of proclaiming, 'In forty days Ninveh will be overthrown,' when the people of Ninveh believed God. They proclaimed a fast and put on sackcloth, from the greatest of them to the least. When the news reached the king of Ninveh, he got up from his throne, took off his robe, put on sackcloth and sat in ashes. He then had this proclamation made throughout Ninveh: "By decree . . . they are to cry out to God with all their might – let each of them turn from his evil way and from the violence they practice* (Jonah 3:3-8).

Was it the power with which Jonah preached? The forty-day deadline definitely would have put some urgency into the message. We don't really know how he preached, but we do know his message was repent or be overthrown, and the people accepted God's word.

In our culture, fire-and-brimstone preaching has been criticized. Many believe that it's a type of scare tactic that frightens people into making a profession of faith without any repentance or heartfelt change. Because of this, some only encourage people to say a little prayer, and everything will be okay. This is the other extreme and produces no change in attitude or behavior and no passionate love for God or His Word. Something is missing.

The path to a balanced biblical message is to understand God, His plan, and His love for us. Our God is absolutely good and worthy of all our praise. From the beginning, He had a plan for man to live a certain way, but He also had a plan to save man when he failed. His very nature and His plan are perfect examples of His love for us. He is the God who was, the God who is, and the God who will come again. By understanding that, we are better equipped to grow, live a life for God, and put the words found in Romans 12:1-2 into practice. *I exhort you, therefore, brothers, in view of God's mercies, to offer yourselves as a sacrifice, living and set apart for God. This will please him; it is the logical "Temple worship" for you. In other words, do not let yourselves be conformed to the standards of the 'olam hazeh* [this present age, world]. *Instead, keep letting yourselves be transformed by the renewing of your minds; so that you will know what God wants and will agree that what he wants is good, satisfying and able to succeed.*

Chapter 1

Our Need to Refocus

What Do I Have to Do?

What must I do to have eternal life? Eternal life is almost an incomprehensible concept. As I meditated on this, I realized how insufficient my works are. I thought about how God has reached down through the generations to me, to you, to all of us. I wondered what my part in His plan might be. God gives us thoughts like these to mull over in our minds, but He's also given us His Word to teach us.

> *A man approached Yeshua [Jesus] and said, "Rabbi, what good thing should I do in order to have eternal life?" He said to him, "Why are you asking me about good? There is One who is good! But if you want to obtain eternal life, observe the mitzvot [command-ments]." The man asked him, "Which ones?" and Yeshua said, "Don't murder, don't commit adultery,*

don't steal, don't give false testimony, honor father
and mother and love your neighbor as yourself."
The young man said to him, "I have kept all these;
where do I still fall short?" Yeshua said to him, "If
you are serious about reaching the goal, go and
sell your possessions, give to the poor, and you will
have riches in heaven. Then come, follow me!" But
when the young man heard this, he went away sad,
because he was wealthy. (Matthew 19:16-22)

This same occasion is described in Mark 10 and Luke 18 where the man called Yeshua *Good Rabbi* [Master]. This story is repeated because each gospel was written to a different audience, and each contains a different purpose or perspective.

The gospel of Matthew was written specifically to the Jewish people. It contains a rich Jewish genealogy and repeatedly speaks about Yeshua being the prophesied Messiah, the King of Israel. Matthew shows us the relationship of Yeshua to the Law and Old Testament prophets. He encouraged the Jewish people to see their heritage in the context of a greater law and their history in the light of the spiritual kingdom of God. He didn't believe the Scriptures lost their significance as Yeshua fulfilled them. Rather, the Hebrew Scriptures gained significance through Yeshua.

The dramatic book of Mark is short and action packed. Mark was more concerned with telling about the events than the timetable of the events, and he used words like *immediately* and *at once* to portray a fast-moving story. His account is strong on miracles and spoke to the Roman people. They were looking for a "bullock" as the perfect leader. To the tough Roman people, enduring death and suffering were signs of strength and power, so they waited for a suffering servant. Mark used great detail to describe the suffering, death, and resurrection to help them comprehend who Yeshua is.

Like Matthew, Luke gave us Yeshua's genealogy and recorded events of His earthly life to establish Him as a true historical personality. Luke told about Yeshua's compassion and His heart as He brought good news to the poor, sight to the blind, and freedom to the oppressed. We see that Yeshua became one of us and lived a perfect life for all to see. In this way, Luke spoke to the Greeks, because they were focused on being perfect, and they were looking for a perfect man.

John is the universal gospel. He covered the smallest time segment of Yeshua's earthly life, but detailed for us who Yeshua was, where He came from, and what He came to do. The first three gospels speak of the kingdom of God, but John's gospel tells of God's love and His gift of eternal life in simple-enough language to be understood by everyone. John told us that Yeshua said, *Whoever hears what I am saying and trusts the One who sent me has eternal life – that is, he will not come up for judgment but has already crossed over from death to life!* (John 5:24). He indicated that eternal life was to be experienced here and now. So, each gospel gives us a different perspective of the earthly life of Yeshua.

The story of the man who inquired about eternal life appears essentially the same in the first three gospels. Mark said, *As he [Yeshua] was starting on his way, a man ran up, kneeled down in front of him and asked, "Good rabbi, what should I do to obtain eternal life?"* (Mark 10:17). In Luke, we read, *One of the leaders asked him, "Good rabbi, what should I do to obtain eternal life?"* (Luke 18:18). This man asked what he should *do*. He had no concept of eternal life, because he was only looking to *do* something, which we tend to do even after we're saved. The word *do* indicates an act. It's an achievement, something we attain and can say we've done. Sadly, it also means "a performance."

I was always performance oriented. My dad was a highly decorated World War II veteran, an Army Ranger, and a Purple Heart recipient; he was awarded the Bronze Star for bravery. He was a very dedicated father and a wonderful husband to my mom. However, being ten years of age when the great depression of 1929 hit didn't afford him the childhood or the opportunities that many of us experience in a prosperous society like ours today. Therefore, he lived vicariously through me. I was the last of four children and the only boy. He wanted me to be the straight-A student, the gifted athlete, and the quintessential success story. So I became performance oriented.

Even after my encounter with the Lord, I performed. It was in no shape or form malicious, but it was exhausting. I shared the gospel everywhere and anywhere. I read my Bible all the time and prayed constantly. I was always doing for the Lord. Maybe I was subconsciously trying to prove to God that I was worthy of His sacrifice. Whatever the case, I guess I did not fully understand the grace of God. Truth be told, I still struggle with this today, as I think God's love is something to be earned.

Likewise, this man came to Yeshua and asked, *"What good thing should I do in order to have eternal life?"* His interest was in how to get something. He wanted to know what he had to do. He was obviously wealthy; maybe he thought he could buy himself into heaven. Maybe he offered to give money to the synagogue. We don't know, but he wanted to do something to be entitled to eternal life.

Are we entitled to *anything*? If we're entitled to a free education, we'd be fools not to take advantage of it. But even our education isn't free. It costs the taxpayers. So, it's a privilege. Everything is a privilege – especially eternal life. This man who came to Yeshua didn't understand that eternal life isn't earned. He wanted to obtain it, but he hadn't even come to the realization that Yeshua was Messiah. He only knew Him as a Jewish man who was a good rabbi.

Can We Understand *Eternal Life*?

If we look at the word *eternal* in a Greek lexicon, it means "without end, never to cease, or everlasting." The root word for eternal in the Greek means "forever," which really drives the point home. *Life* is the state of one who is breathing and has a beating heart. When these stop, the person's life is over.

Three synonyms for *eternal* are *deathless*, *timeless*, and *ageless*. Think about being ageless for a moment. As a people, especially in America, we are enamored with living forever. Americans spend billions on anti-aging formulas, but the truth is that at some point we're all going to get wrinkles. We're aging at this very moment; there's no way around it.

> To die is gain, but we do everything we can to stay alive.

But at the same time, we're obsessed with living forever. We like to quote the apostle Paul and say, *to die is gain*, but we do everything we can to stay alive (Philippians 1:21).

There seems to be a dichotomy or paradox here. Remember the Fountain of Youth? This spring of water was supposed to restore the youth of anyone who drank from it. In the fifth century BC, Herodotus, father of modern-day history and contemporary of Socrates, made it famous.[2] But the legend of the Fountain of Youth became prominent again in 1513, when

---

2   *en.wikipedia.org/wiki/Fountain_of_Youth.*

Juan Ponce De León, the first governor of Puerto Rico, decided to go to Florida. He went to St. Augustine, presently the oldest city in America, looking for the Fountain of Youth. Today, Florida seems to be God's waiting room and anything but the Fountain of Youth. When people retire, they go to Florida to spend their last years in the sun. But we know this fountain isn't in Florida. The real Fountain of Youth is the living waters of God's Spirit. We know this, but we don't always focus on it or live by it.

Why are we so obsessed with living forever? We can gain some insight in the book of Ecclesiastes. We can't take everything in this book as God's words for us to follow because Solomon wrote much of it when he was jaded. Solomon wrote, *So I recommend enjoyment – a person can do nothing better under the sun than eat, drink and enjoy himself; this is what should accompany him as he does his work for as long as God gives him to live under the sun* (Ecclesiastes 8:15).

He'll be there for us, but He has the perfect plan, not us.

When we see instruction like this, we must recognize that it's not God telling us to do that. Solomon was weary, worn out, or dulled by overindulgence when he wrote that.

Truth from Ecclesiastes says, *For everything there is a season* (Ecclesiastes 3:1). God is a God of timing; at just the right time, He sent Yeshua. We can't do anything right if the time is wrong. Timing is crucial, but it's very hard to find our timing in the spiritual realm. Is it time to leave or time to stay? Is it time to serve in this ministry or that ministry? And most of the time we operate on emotions. If we want something bad enough, we try to get God to agree with us. Then we interpret it as God leading us, but it's really us leading Him. We're saying, "Come on, God, bless my efforts." He'll be there for us, but He has the perfect plan, not us. So, we have to be careful with our emotions. We can't trust our heart, because it's evil above all things. *The heart is more deceitful than anything else and mortally sick. Who can fathom it?* (Jeremiah 17:9). *He has made everything suited to its time,* and it's best if we recognize His timing (Ecclesiastes 3:11).

We also know that God *has given human beings an awareness of eternity; but in such a way that they can't fully comprehend, from beginning to end, the things God does* (Ecclesiastes 3:11). We have an inborn desire to find Him and eternity, but it's a struggle. God has planted eternity in every one of our hearts. Our soul is everlasting, but our bodies are not. We know this on a deep level, but we struggle to comprehend it. We're wired for it, but because our lives are finite and we're linear, we can't fully grasp it.

If we draw out a time line, we make a straight line and fill in dates and events. We never draw a time line that looks like a sine wave which oscillates up and down; ours is always straight. We know when a person is born; when they die, we say, "Oh, they're with the Father," but we can't fully comprehend what we've said. If God can help us comprehend just a little bit more, it would help us live toward that goal, as opposed to living for the here and now.

Hebrews 2:14-15 says, *Therefore, since the children share a common physical nature as human beings, he became like them and shared that same human nature; so that by his death he might render ineffective the one who had power over death (that is, the Adversary) and thus set free those who had been in bondage all their lives because of their fear of death.*

This tells us we're all related. We may have cultural differences, but we're all human beings. We might even become racially blind, because we have incredible similarities. Human beings are looking for peace and solace and trying to figure out their direction in life. They want the best for their families, and they're suckers for love. Since we share a common physical nature, *he became like them.* This obviously refers to the Messiah, and he *shared that same human nature.* He may have been a superman, but He was still all man. So when He suffered, He suffered as a man; when He was tired, He was tired as a man. His flogging, those nails, and His crucifixion were very, very painful, *so that by his death he might render ineffective the one who had power over death (that is, the Adversary) and thus set free those who had been in bondage all their lives because of their fear of death.*

The writer of Hebrews acknowledges in this book to Jewish believers that the fear of death is very normal, very natural, and very human. He's also saying that this fear of death has held men in lifelong bondage.

Look at this word *fear*: it's the Greek word *phobeo,* from which we get the word *phobia* in our English language. It means "that which strikes terror" or "to be terrified," as opposed to being a little nervous. He's saying that the cross – the crucifixion, the execution stake, the sacrificial death of the Messiah – was supposed to free us from this misery.

We don't think about eternity much when we're young, because we have our whole life ahead of us. But as the chapters turn, we stop to think about the reality of death, especially with today's media describing all of the world's sickness and sorrow. However, if the sacrifice of Messiah was supposed to free us from this misery, why are we still so tormented? Maybe, just maybe, it's because we're not totally sure, because we can't fully comprehend eternal life. We talk about it and believe it spiritually, theologically, and theoretically, but we don't necessarily believe it in the same concrete way that we believe when we're sitting in a room talking to each other. What if we're wrong? We don't have scientific, hands-on proof that we can see and touch. What if it's not true?

Our Focus

How do we adequately address these questions? First of all, the Bible is clear that if this is all there is, we are to be pitied more than any other person on the face of the planet. *If it is only for this life that we have put our hope in the Messiah, we are more pitiable than anyone* (1 Corinthians 15:19). Maybe we're so unsure of the eternal that we get obsessed with our lives in the here and now.

While I was thinking about this, I had some thoughts about television. We use a DVD player instead of cable. Years ago, we had cable, but I got rid of it when our eldest son was young. We had been watching some cartoons, when a commercial came on for a program where they showed a head getting chopped off. That was it. I pulled the cable.

> Maybe we're so unsure of the eternal that we get obsessed with our lives in the here and now.

However, recently we were on vacation and stayed in a place that had cable TV with 1,139 channels. Imagine that! And I couldn't find anything to watch. Finally, after channel surfing I stumbled upon something they call WFC – the World Fashion Channel. Twenty-four hours a day it talks about fashion. Then I found TFN – The Food Network. Every kind of food fixed a million ways from everywhere in the world. Now, there's nothing wrong with fashion and food. We all get dressed in the morning and need food to keep going.

The next channel that grabbed me was HGTV. All day long, they renovated and flipped house after house; they were flippin' and floppin' and flippin' and floppin' those houses like a game of Twister. But it was no game; the whole network, 24/7, was about home remodeling. Basically, those three channels said my clothes, my food, and my house weren't good enough. They implied I needed, or even deserved, something better.

Then we go into stores and receive subliminal messages. Little voices bombard us with ideas that we need bigger TV screens, more advanced technology, and nicer furniture and fixtures. These things aren't wrong in and of themselves, but they can become idols. I want to understand God's heart on these issues and at the same time not become overly obsessive. However, when we look at Yeshua, the apostles, or other great men and women of God, they seem to be pretty obsessive.

Even though the Food Network seems to obsess over food, eating is a mainstay everywhere around the world, even if a small dish of rice is the only food shared. It's communal. This intimate fellowship is a very important part of a close-knit culture. Even after the resurrection, Yeshua asked for fish at the Sea of Galilee.

Just as day was breaking, Yeshua stood on shore, but the talmidim [disciples] didn't know it was he. He said to them, "You don't have any fish, do you?"

"No," they answered him.

He said to them, "Throw in your net to starboard

*and you will catch some." So they threw in their net,
and there were so many fish in it that they couldn't
haul it aboard . . . When they stepped ashore, they
saw a fire of burning coals with a fish on it, and
some bread.* (John 21:4-6, 9)

Sharing that food was an important activity for them.

However, prior to that time, Yeshua gave a single sermon
where He started with the preamble in Matthew 5, went on to
teach the Torah in Matthew 6, and then gave a lot of warnings
in Matthew 7. It was all one sermon. In the middle we find a
verse where He said, *Therefore, I tell you, don't worry about
your life – what you will eat or drink; or about your body –
what you will wear. Isn't life more than food and the body more
than clothing?* (Matthew 6:25). Isn't it incredible that we have
all these television channels devoted to this stuff, and He said
not to worry about any of it?

Yeshua wasn't taking issue with what we eat or wear, because
He knows we need these things, and we must make plans. The
issue isn't focusing on what we will eat or wear today, but on
what we will eat or wear twenty or
thirty years from now. Such worry
about the future is sin because it denies
the love, wisdom, and power of God.
It denies the love of God by implying that He doesn't care about us. It
denies His wisdom by implying that

> God did not create us in
> His image with no higher
> destiny than that we
> should consume food.

He doesn't know what He is doing. And it denies His power by
implying that He isn't able to provide for our needs. This type
of worry causes us to devote our finest energies to making sure
that we will have enough to live on. Then before we know it,

our lives have passed, and we have missed the central purpose for which we were made. God did not create us in His image with no higher destiny than that we should consume food. We are here to love, worship, and serve Him and to represent His interests on earth. Our bodies are intended to be our servants, not our masters.

Consider what Yeshua said in Matthew 8:19-20 regarding these things we worry about: *A Torah-teacher approached and said to him, "Rabbi, I will follow you wherever you go." Yeshua said to him, "The foxes have holes, and the birds flying about have nests, but the Son of Man has no home of his own."*

This teacher had good intentions without a malicious heart. If we read the gospel accounts, we see that Yeshua always spoke about the cost of following Him. He never mentioned the rewards until the very end, so Peter got incredibly frustrated. Yeshua was forthright and honest in letting them know it would cost them everything to follow Him.

Today, we seldom talk about the costs. We mostly talk about the rewards. This is a mistake and not fair because it's not the whole truth. Then, when we start following Him and things fall apart, we ask, "What's happening?"

Peter reminded the people when he said, *Dear friends, don't regard as strange the fiery ordeal occurring among you to test you, as if something extraordinary were happening to you. Rather, to the extent that you share the fellowship of the Messiah's sufferings, rejoice; so that you will rejoice even more when his Sh'khinah* [dwelling, glory] *is revealed* (1 Peter 4:12-13).

Yeshua had no home, but He wasn't saying we shouldn't have a home. In actuality, He wasn't homeless. He chose to not have a home of his own, because He didn't need one. He was always moving. This gave Him a chance to share with people when He went into their homes. He stayed with friends and ministered to them and their families. He had work to do, and He couldn't rest until it was accomplished.

He asked this teacher if he knew what it would take to follow Him. The same is true for us. The world isn't our resting place even though we have comfortable homes, shoes, and beds. But things that are too nice can take control of us. Once things start to control us, we take our focus off the One who should be controlling us.

The world isn't our resting place.

In considering these television channels and what they do to us, we can see just how self-absorbed we've become. Think about it. We have iPhones, YouTube, Twitter, and Facebook. We have our faces in everyone else's book except His. Yet, Yeshua told His followers exactly what it would take to follow Him. *Then Yeshua told his talmidim* [disciples], *"If anyone wants to come after me, let him say 'No' to himself, take up his execution-stake* [cross], *and keep following me"* (Matthew 16:24).

He was a rabbi; that's what the disciples knew. Many rabbis walked the land, and each had his own students – not many, only ten, twelve, or maybe only five. They taught outside under the trees, and their followers walked with them. It was called "walking in the footsteps" of the rabbi. Sometimes they walked so close dust from the rabbi's sandals would hit them. They watched everything their rabbi did, because they were being "marinated." They were soaking up every teaching they heard.

Notice that Yeshua asked if anyone wanted to come after Him, to follow Him, or to be His disciple. He didn't ask if anyone wanted to get saved. That was assumed, a no-brainer. But just making a verbal statement of faith and being baptized isn't salvation. Many people, particularly the young, don't understand repentance and being immersed in the Word. When Yeshua told them to go out, make disciples, and baptize them, He wasn't only talking about water. He was telling them to immerse their disciples in the reality that there is a Father, there is a prophesied Messiah who connected them to the Father, and there is a Holy Spirit dwelling in their tabernacle.

Sometimes an ornery, miserable, satanically influenced person will get saved, and we can see a new light in their eyes. We see an absolute, positive, legitimate, obvious transformation, and it's as real as can be, and that is what matters. Yeshua said that if anyone wanted to follow Him, he should

We're called to be bondservants.

deny himself, take up his execution stake, and keep following. That meant it wouldn't be a one-time profession, but it was going to be a long-distance, rest-of-their-lives, constant following. It may mean falling, repenting, getting back up, following, and falling again – over and over for their whole lives.

We need to look at the word *deny* to understand what Yeshua was saying to them. It means to forget oneself. It's not the same as self-denial. That's giving things up to show God we're good people. What He's talking about here is the act of restraining one's own desires. It means we have no rights. What? If He's saying we have no rights, He's basically saying, we're called to be bondservants. Are we supposed to be bondservants?

We tend to think maybe Paul was supposed to be a bondservant, because he was the great apostle Paul. In reality, we're all called to be bondservants of the Master Yeshua. As far as masters and taskmasters go, we could never find a better one. He will give us plenty of times of refreshing, and He will change our lives for the better. We'll be happier than we've ever been, so we can trust being enslaved to Him. Peter tells us to *submit as people who are free, but not letting your freedom serve as an excuse for evil; rather, submit as God's slaves* (1 Peter 2:16).

The Perpetual Offering

By looking at the perpetual offering in Exodus and recognizing Yeshua in it, we can see the hand of God in the timing and complexity of His salvation. From this sacrifice, we can realize that eternal life is legitimate, really legitimate, and we can live for it. When Yeshua taught, He said we shouldn't make our offering *corban*, a gift to God, instead of helping our parents. He told them to *honor your father and your mother* (Mark 7:10).

Corban means a sacrifice to God. How much do we sacrifice? We sacrifice our time, our money, and our energy. We sacrifice our families, our sanity, and our bodies. We sacrifice our minds as we lose our minds over things. We sacrifice our emotions and, sadly, our very hearts. We tie our hearts to the things that can destroy us. Why do we do this? For personal enjoyment? To climb the corporate ladder? And when we make it to the top, then what? There seems to be no satiation point.

The root of the word *offering* is *karov*. This is the enlightening aspect of the word *offering*. It means "to come near, to approach, or to join in." The sacrificial system of the Torah provided the means for us to draw near to God. It wasn't simply an atonement for sin, but it was like an invitation to be close to the Father. The whole system is quite detailed in the first seven chapters of Leviticus where we read about five distinct offerings. God had a reason for all of the detail.

The eternal, perpetual offering had to be made every day. God was saturating His people with sacrifices so, one day, they wouldn't miss out on the ultimate sacrifice.

ADONAI said to Moshe [Moses], *"Give an order to the people of Isra'el. Tell them, 'You are to take care to offer me at the proper time the food presented to me as offerings made by fire, providing a fragrant aroma for me.'* (Numbers 28:1-2)

This was not a suggestion; it was an order, a command, to the people of Israel, the children of God. This offering wasn't to be just at the proper time or according to the specific details. God was looking for a sacrifice. He wasn't looking for just a grain or fellowship offering. God wanted a sacrifice that provided *a fragrant aroma*. In most other Bible versions, God said that the offerings, the sacrifices, are His food, His sustenance. We know He is Spirit, so we aren't talking about carbs, protein, and fat. That's all food; it's what keeps us alive. He's saying that what keeps Him going are the offerings. They are what sustains Him. Numbers 28:3 says, *Tell them, 'This is the offering made by fire that you are to bring to ADONAI: male lambs in their first year and without defect, two daily as a regular burnt offering.'*

This was called the eternal or perpetual offering. Many people believe that in the Old Testament when the Jews sinned they had to bring an offering to the temple, but they'd never be able to leave. It's actually a myth that every time they sinned they had to offer a sacrifice. In reality, most individuals bought the sacrifices for the three annual festivals. They had money changers, so they wouldn't have to carry a lamb from far away. They brought money, exchanged it for local currency, and bought an animal for sacrifice.

According to Exodus 23:14-17, there are three annual festivals – Passover, Shavuot (Festival of Weeks or Pentecost), and Sukkot (Feast of Booths or Tabernacles). Those were the three festivals, known as Shelosh Regalim. These are festivals within the festivals which talk about the God who was, the God who is, and the God who will be. In other words, the "God who was" is the Passover Lamb; the "God who is" is the Holy Spirit that came during Shavuot and is dwelling in us; and the "God who will be" is the glorified One when He returns to set up His kingdom on earth as it is in heaven during Sukkot. These were the times when the Jewish people came and offered sacrifices.

However, the Levites offered sacrifices every single, solitary day, one in the morning and one in the afternoon; it was the perpetual offering. Why? Because those sacrifices kept the sanctuary clean, so God could dwell there. The sacrifices for the sins of the entire nation of Israel were offered twice a day, every day, so the manifest presence of God could reside in the Holy of Holies. God's presence, His unapproachable light, cannot be around sin, so they had to provide these daily sacrifices in order to keep His presence there. Exodus tells us about this perpetual sacrifice:

> *Now this is what you are to offer on the altar: two lambs a year old, regularly, every day. The one lamb you are to offer in the morning and the other lamb at dusk . . . Through all your generations this is to be the regular burnt offering at the entrance to the tent of meeting before* ADONAI. *There is where I will meet with you to speak with you. There I will meet with the people of Isra'el; and the place will be consecrated by my glory.* (Exodus 29:38-39, 42-43)

This describes a perpetual sacrifice, the eternal offering, one lamb offered in the morning and the other at dusk as burnt offerings in the temple. So, as long as they kept the offerings, God would meet and speak with them. Who doesn't want to meet with the Lord? He said He'd meet with them and speak to them, but the sins of the people pollute the temple and the altar. Sins are airborne, and they pollute the entire world. The sacrifices cleansed the sanctuary, and with this regular cleansing, the people could avoid defiling the sanctuary, and God's presence would not depart. This cleansing offering was the perpetual sacrifice, and it was a constant reminder to the people, because it happened every single day.

The Torah doesn't tell us about the timing of this sacrifice, but it's supported by the Talmud and other writings. The Mishnah Tamid 3:7 says nine o'clock **Yeshua is the** in the morning and three o'clock **perpetual sacrifice.** in the afternoon. Josephus, who is highly regarded as a historian, wrote *The Antiquities of the Jews.* He wrote from the death of Queen Alexandra to the death of Antigonus (Volume 14, page 3) and stated that the sacrifices were at nine o'clock and three o'clock. Philo of Alexandria, who wrote in AD 20, also known as Philo Judaeus, was a Jewish philosopher. In his book *The Special Laws* (Volume 1, page 169), he said the sacrifices were at nine o'clock and three o'clock.

Do those times remind you of anything? Yeshua is the perpetual sacrifice. In the gospel of Mark we read, *Then they nailed him to the execution stake; and they divided his clothes among themselves, throwing dice to determine what each man should get. It was nine in the morning when they nailed him to the stake . . . At noon, darkness covered the whole Land until three o'clock in the afternoon. At three, he uttered a loud cry, "Elohi! Elohi! L'mah sh'vaktani?" (which means, "My God! My*

God! Why have you deserted me?") On hearing this, some of the bystanders said, "Look! He's calling for Eliyahu!" One ran and soaked a sponge in vinegar, put it on a stick and gave it to him to drink. "Wait!" he said, "Let's see if Eliyahu will come and take him down." But Yeshua let out a loud cry and gave up his spirit (Mark 15:24-25, 33-37). The eternal sacrifice that the priests offered every single day portrayed the sacrifice of Yeshua, which came hundreds of years later.

Could God, who is complex in His unity, sit enthroned in heaven and, at the same time, fill the universe with His presence? Could He exist infinite and uncontainable in His majesty and, at the same time, manifest His glory among us in the tent of a human being? Is that possible? According to the Bible, anything is possible with God. In Luke, the question was answered when the angel told Mary about Elizabeth expecting a child. The angel stated, *For with God, nothing is impossible* (Luke 1:37). Remember Sarah? Her womb was old and nonfunctional, and Abraham wasn't in his prime either. They both laughed as they were told they'd have a child at that time the following year. But God asked, *Is anything too hard for ADONAI?* (Genesis 18:14).

In Genesis 18, they didn't know God very well, but as they got to know Him, they started to change. Their faith was becoming powerful. Note what the ArtScroll Siddur, Jewish commentary to Psalm 91, says: "At the moment that Moses finished building the Tabernacle, a question arose: How could a Tabernacle with walls and curtains contain the Presence of the Almighty? The Master of the Universe Himself explained, 'The entire world cannot contain My glory, yet when I wish, I can concentrate My entire essence into one small spot. Indeed, I am Most High, yet I sit in a refuge – in the shadow of the Tabernacle.'"

Why is it so hard to believe that if He could sit in the refuge of a tabernacle, He can sit in the refuge of a human being? God's unveiled glory is a consuming fire. He's not someone to be toyed with. God is infinite. He can manifest the fullness of His glory in a specific place in time and space and still be infinite and uncontainable at the same time.

If we look at Exodus 24:9-11, it says, *Moshe* [Moses], *Aharon* [Aaron], *Nadav* [Nadab], *Avihu* [Abihu], *and seventy of the leaders of Israel went up; and they saw the God of Isra'el. Under his feet was something like a sapphire stone pavement as clear as the sky itself. He did not reach out his hand against these notables of Isra'el; on the contrary, they saw God, even as they were eating and drinking.* They went up the mountain, *and they saw the God of Isra'el.* Saw the God of Israel? And *Under his feet was something like a sapphire stone pavement –* feet? This isn't hard to embrace. It paints a picture of Yeshua as Lord, as Messiah, as God in the flesh. It's all throughout the Bible. *He did not reach out his hand against these notables of Isra'el . . . they saw God, even as they were eating and drinking.*

He's not someone to be toyed with.

If it required a sacrifice every morning and every evening of a one-year-old male lamb without spot or blemish as a burnt offering to maintain a manifest presence of the Lord in the Holy of Holies of the temple, so that one man, from one family, from one tribe, on one day of the year could make atonement for himself and all of Israel, then what kind of sacrifice would it require to allow all men to come boldly into the very throne room and presence of almighty God? And then to not only have a personal, deep, intimate, one-on-one relationship with the Father, but to also have His Holy Spirit dwell in our tabernacles? God paid an immeasurable, incomparable, priceless price because He doesn't want anyone to perish. He wants none left behind.[3] *The Lord is not slow in keeping his promise, as some people think of slowness; on the contrary, he is patient with you; for it is not his purpose that anyone should be destroyed, but that everyone should turn from his sins* (2 Peter 3:9). Maybe, just maybe, God really wants us to dwell with Him forever.

---

3   In Israel, when they train in the military, the one who gets there first has to make sure the last one gets there. He has to go out and get the last one if necessary.

Chapter 2

We Live by Trust, Not by What We See

We Walk by Faith

One time, I spoke to someone who was close to dying, and she told me she was scared. That took courage, because most people won't admit to being scared. Fear is a normal and understandable response when we're faced with the reality of our own mortality and have no hope of anything beyond this life. But we believe in something more. We are doing a faith walk where we don't physically see what we believe. We walk by faith, and not by sight. Second Corinthians 5:7 says, *for we live by trust, not by what we see.* Even though we trust this is the truth, it still causes some anxiety for many of us.

To our human minds, what we believe seems kind of wild, almost crazy, or unbelievable. Somehow, God impregnated a young Jewish girl. *The angel said to her, "Don't be afraid, Miryam* [Mary], *for you have found favor with God. Look! You will become pregnant, you will give birth to a son, and you are to name him Yeshua"* (Luke 1:30-31). This young Jewish girl was probably no more than fourteen or fifteen years of age, and she gave birth to a normal human being who never sinned in His thirty-three years of life. Never! Not even in His thoughts. Imagine that. Even when we try not to sin, we fail. He was thirty-three and had never sinned. Then

We walk by faith, trusting God.

He died, was buried, and preserved from decomposition for three days. Somehow, the giant stone was rolled away from His tomb, and He rose from the dead. He ascended in bodily form and sat down at the right hand of God. *So then, after he had spoken to them, the Lord Yeshua was taken up into heaven and sat at the right hand of God* (Mark 16:19).

In the future, He's going to come back, restore the heavens and the earth, and give us new bodies. He encourages us in 2 Peter 3:13 by saying, *but we, following along with his promise, wait for new heavens and a new earth, in which righteousness will be at home.* He has promised this, and we believe it, but in our human minds, it's a stretch.

Yes, we walk by faith, trusting God, and not what we see, but God has prepared our hearts and minds to recognize His provision for us. As I mentioned earlier, the Lord gave Moses very specific instructions to give to the priests.

> *Now this is what you are to offer on the altar: two lambs a year old, regularly, every day. The one lamb you are to offer in the morning and the other lamb at dusk. Through all your generations this is to be the regular burnt offering at the entrance to the tent*

of meeting before ADONAI. There is where I will meet with you to speak with you. (Exodus 29:38-39, 42)

The sacrifice had to be offered, one in the morning and one in the evening, at nine o'clock in the morning and three o'clock in the afternoon. Every morning and every evening a sacrifice of a one-year-old male lamb without spot or blemish had to be offered to maintain a manifest presence of the Lord in the Holy of Holies. This was known as the eternal or perpetual offering.

This offering had to take place, because God is perfect and cannot be around sin. If the priests failed to obey this command, the presence of God would have departed like it did in Ezekiel's time (Ezekiel 8-10). This perpetual sacrifice wasn't maintained to keep a little manifest presence but to come into the presence. And it not only provided a way to enter into His presence to bring offerings but to also have an intimate, personal, one-on-one relationship with almighty God, the Creator and Sustainer of the universe and be able to call him Abba Father.

Ultimately, man's tabernacle would become the Holy of Holies, and he would house the manifest presence of God in his body – the Spirit of God would live inside man. This never happened in the Old Testament; the Spirit came on people, but He never resided in people. Even though this is an amazing act by God toward believers, many Christians, who are raised in the faith and have learned about the indwelling Holy Spirit, have become complacent and apathetic to this great truth. I call this dry-eyed Christianity, and it's flagrant. First Corinthians 3:16 clarifies this concept. *Don't you know that you people are God's temple and that God's Spirit lives in you?*

Abrahamic Covenant

To fully understand the magnificent truth of the Spirit dwelling in man, we need to go back to the source. The New Testament only provides us with very little of the detail we need – just one sentence: Yeshua was flogged and crucified. This doesn't go deep enough, so we don't go deep enough. We need to go back to Genesis 15 where the Lord made His covenant promise to Abram: *Some time later the word of* Adonai *came to Avram* [Abram] *in a vision.* Some time later? Later than what? We need to know what *later* means here. We need the context.

There are five principles to the hermeneutics of studying and understanding Scripture, and the most important of these five is context – text taken out of context is pretext. Unless we know what's happening, we won't understand. For example, when we read Paul's letter to the Philippians, we need to know who the Philippians are and who Paul is. We need to know where Paul was when he wrote the letter, where the Philippians were when they received it, and what was going on in Philippi at the time.

So, what does *some time later* mean? Well, some time later than Genesis 14 when a great war was fought amongst the kings. When five kings came out to Siddim Valley to fight against four kings, the city of Sodom fell, and Lot, Abram's nephew, was captured. After Abram heard of Lot's capture, he took 318 men with him and pursued the attacking kings. During the night, Abram and his servants divided their forces and attacked the king of Persia. Abram recovered all the plundered goods and brought Lot back home, along with the women and other people. After the battle, Abram was tested when the king of Sodom said, *Give me the people, and keep the goods for yourself* (Genesis 14:21).

But Abram replied, *"I have raised my hand in an oath to*

ADONAI, El 'Elyon, maker of heaven and earth, that I will not take so much as a thread or a sandal thong of anything that is yours; so that you won't be able to say, 'I made Avram rich'" (Genesis 14:22-23). Abram wanted to depend totally on the Lord. Do you know why he was called the friend of God? Because Abram had proven himself obedient, and God could depend on him. This is what the *some time later* refers to.

> Some time later the word of ADONAI came to Avram in a vision: "Don't be afraid, Avram. I am your protector; your reward will be very great."
>
> Avram replied, "ADONAI, God, what good will your gifts be to me if I continue childless; and Eli'ezer from Dammesek [Damascus] inherits my possessions? You haven't given me a child," Avram continued, "so someone born in my house will be my heir."
>
> But the word of ADONAI came to him: "This man will not be your heir. No, your heir will be a child from your own body." Then he brought him outside and said, "Look up at the sky, and count the stars – if you can count them! Your descendants will be that many!"
>
> He believed in ADONAI, and he credited it to him as righteousness. (Genesis 15:1-6)

First, the Lord reassured Abram and told him He would protect him and give him a reward, but Abram reminded the Lord that he had no heir and suggested a stranger in his home would become his heir. The Lord corrected Abram and told him the heir would be his own child, and his descendants would be as numerous as the stars. Even in his old age, Abram believed God, and his faith made him righteous.

> *Then he said to him, "I am ADONAI, who brought you out from Ur-Kasdim* [Ur of the Chaldees] *to give you this land as your possession."*
>
> *He replied, "ADONAI, God, how am I to know that I will possess it?"* (Genesis 15:7-8)

So, Abram asked God for a sign; he was free to do this because he was talking to his Father. To understand, we need to go back to the first theocratic covenant. There are five theocratic covenants in the Bible: the Abrahamic covenant, the Mosaic covenant, the Israeli covenant, the Davidic covenant, and the new covenant. They're all made with the children of Israel, even the new covenant. Jeremiah 31:30 says, *"Here, the days are coming," says ADONAI, "when I will make a new covenant with the house of Isra'el and the house of Y'hudah* [Judah]."

The Abrahamic covenant in Genesis 12 is the most important covenant, because God was initiating the promise there. It had to be initiated before it could be fulfilled. In Scripture, this follows the Tower of Babel and is the glorious turning point for the human kingdom. It's the first and most important theocratic covenant. Father Abraham is the father of Judaism, the father of Christianity, and the father of Islam – the three major religions in the world. *Now ADONAI said to Avram, "Get yourself out of your country"* (Genesis 12:1).

Abram was living in southeast Iraq on the Persian Gulf in

Mesopotamia in a city called Ur at this time. He may have been on the Gulf because he was very rich. We know that Terah, Abram's father, worshipped other gods, and Jewish tradition indicates that he was an idol maker. In a pagan society, idol makers do very well. *Y'hoshua said to all the people, "This is what ADONAI the God of Isra'el says: 'In antiquity your ancestors lived on the other side of the [Euphrates] River — Terach the father of Avraham and Nachor — and they served other gods* (Joshua 24:2). Archeologists have uncovered what they believe to be his house, which even had indoor plumbing.[4] They lived in a pagan country and life was good, but God said to Abram, *"Get yourself out of your country, away from your kinsmen and away from your father's house, and go to the land*

> The nation of Israel would become a channel of blessing to the entire world by bringing forth the Messiah – a universal blessing.

that I will show you. I will make of you a great nation, I will bless you, and I will make your name great; and you are to be a blessing. I will bless those who bless you, but I will curse anyone who curses you; and by you all the families of the earth will be blessed" (Genesis 12:1-3).

We see three blessings here, and three is the number for divine perfection; it's the number for God. He said He would make Abram's name great; this is the individual blessing. The national blessing occurs when God promises Abram that he would give birth to a nation. Then, God said He would bless those who blessed him, curse those who cursed him, and by him all the families, everybody in the world, would be blessed. The nation of Israel would become a channel of blessing to

---

4   Sinan Salaheddin, "Home of Abraham, Ur, unearthed by archaeologists in Iraq," *The Christian Science Monitor: www.csmonitor.com/Science/2013/0404/ Home-of-Abraham-Ur-unearthed-by-archaeologists-in-Iraq* (April 4, 2013).

the entire world by bringing forth the Messiah – a universal blessing. So the three blessings are individual, national, and universal in nature.

So, Abram probably wondered how he could become a nation when he didn't even have a single child. He left his father's house, left his land, and traveled to Canaan, but he had no children. He still thought his servant Eliezer from Damascus would inherit his possessions because this was the law of the land. If a man died and had no children, his servant became his heir. Furthermore, Deuteronomy 21:17 explains the law of the right of the firstborn: *He must acknowledge as firstborn the son of the unloved wife by giving him a double portion of everything he owns, for he is the firstfruits of his manhood, and the right of the firstborn is his.* In other words, if a man had four sons, the first one would get 40 percent of the inheritance, and the next three sons would each get 20 percent of the inheritance. Numbers 27:8 makes a provision for the man who dies with no sons but has a daughter: *Moreover, say to the people of Isra'el, 'If a man dies and does not have a son, you are to have his inheritance pass to his daughter.'* God is always looking out for us.

He goes on to say, *If he doesn't have a daughter, give his inheritance to his brothers. If he has no brothers, give his inheritance to his father's brothers. If his father doesn't have brothers, give his inheritance to the closest relative in his family, and he will possess it. This will be the standard for judgment to be used by the people of Isra'el, as* ADONAI *ordered Moshe* (Numbers 27:9-11). Why was God trying to keep this in the family? The purpose of passing the land on was to ensure that the extended family had a means of support and survival. This law was to provide for future generations. In doing this, they blessed one another. That's the way God operates, and we give Him more glory when we see His hand in these details of life. God provides first through people. He wanted His people to provide for their children.

Today, in our culture, we do similar things. We send our children to nice schools and put money aside for college. We are providing for our families in this way. God still wants us to provide for our heirs.

So, in Genesis 15, we can see how good God is. The Lord told Abram not to be afraid. He reassured Abram that He would be his protector, and his reward would be great. He reminded

> We give Him more glory when we see His hand in these details of life.

him that his heir would be his own child. God told Abram to look at the stars and then proclaimed his descendants would be that many. Abram believed God, and it was counted to him as righteousness.

> *Then he said to him, "I am ADONAI, who brought you out from Ur-Kasdim to give you this land as your possession."*

> *He replied, "ADONAI, God, how am I to know that I will possess it?"* (Genesis 15:7-8)

This is where Abram asked for a sign because he wanted to know how he could be sure that he'd possess it. The Lord answered in a seemingly strange, but significant, way. God confirmed His promise with the "cutting" of the covenant.

> *He answered him, "Bring me a three-year-old cow, a three-year-old female goat, a three-year-old ram,*

a dove and a young pigeon." He [Avram] *brought him all these, cut the animals in two and placed the pieces opposite each other; but he didn't cut the birds in half. Birds of prey swooped down on the carcasses, but Avram drove them away.* (Genesis 15:9-11)

We don't really know why the birds weren't cut in half. We can only speculate, but turtle doves and pigeons are peaceful animals, serving as signs of grace and mercy

We know He took in the midst of the cutting of the covenant
the hit for us. and the slaughtering of the animals. God is still full of grace and mercy, and we know He took the hit for us. That's grace and mercy, and maybe it's what He's trying to show us here.

In *The New Order of Priesthood*, David Baron said, "According to the ancient Eastern manner of making a covenant, both the contracting parties passed through the divided pieces of the slain animals, thus symbolically attesting that they pledged their very lives to the fulfillment of the engagement they made."[5]

Abram put those split pieces of the animals opposite each other with the blood dripping from them. Jeremiah also spoke of this type of covenant. God warned Judah and Jerusalem when He said, *As for the men who violated my covenant by not living up to the conditions of the covenant which they made in my presence when they cut the calf in two and passed between its parts – the leaders of Y'hudah* [Judah], *the leaders of Yerushalayim* [Jerusalem], *the officials, the cohanim* [priests] *and all the people of the land who passed between the parts of the calf* (Jeremiah 34:18-19). This wasn't some obscure Mesopotamian covenant

---

5   David Baron, *The New Order of the Priesthood*
     (London: J. Nisbet & Co.).

that God implemented. The people passed between the parts of these blood-dripping animals to pledge themselves to the fulfillment of the covenants.

God told Abram that this was the way He wanted it. His word was everything. Genesis 15 goes on to say, *As the sun was about to set, a deep sleep fell on Avram; horror and great darkness came over him . . . After the sun had set and there was thick darkness, a smoking fire pot and a flaming torch appeared, which passed between these animal parts. That day ADONAI made a covenant with Avram* (Genesis 15:12, 17-18).

We don't know why it was so incredibly dark, but we know Abram fell into a deep sleep. The sun had set, so this was the beginning of a new day, and a smoking fire pot and flaming torch passed between the animal parts. Whenever a covenant or an alliance is made, two parties are needed. But note how many parties are involved here. Abram was asleep, and God passed through the animals. God alone walked through. God alone made the covenant. His presence was symbolized by the fire pot and the flaming torch as they passed through the midst of the pieces of the slain animals. Abram was only a spectator of God's amazing grace.

The fact that God alone passed through the slain animals indicates that the covenant to someday bless all the families of the earth was totally on God and God alone, which made it an unconditional covenant. It was a total covenant of grace, dependent on God to be fulfilled by God. Nothing Abram could do or not do was going to stop God from blessing all the families of the earth. That's why this is the most important covenant.

Not only was this covenant unconditional, but think about all that God had to accomplish to fulfill the promise. After He arranged for Abram to have a son and grandsons, He placed

Joseph in Egypt, so he could be a savior to the Jewish people during the famine. God delivered them from Egypt and led them into Canaan; He delivered them from Babylon and rescued them from the Assyrians, the Medes, the Persians, and the Greeks. And He saved Yeshua from Herod in the first century who was killing all the boys who were two years old and under. Consider all that God has done behind the scenes when we're tempted to think He's indifferent or uninvolved. He's moving pieces around like on a chessboard, and we're usually oblivious to it.

As we return to Genesis 15, we realize it must have taken Abram all day to prepare the animals. It says, *after the sun had set and there was thick darkness.* What happens after the sun sets? *A smoking fire pot and a flaming torch appeared, which passed between these animal parts.* This isn't really hard to interpret, because a smoking fire pot speaks of suffering, like an oven. Might this be likened to the ovens that the Jews were thrown into during World War II? Nobody has been more persecuted than the Jews, and the fire pot represents suffering. We also see a flaming torch. What is that? A flaming torch is a light-bearer. God was saying that this nation, Israel, was going to suffer, but He was also saying that she would be a bearer of light.

He's moving pieces around like on a chessboard, and we're usually oblivious to it.

In John 4, we read about the Samaritan woman at Jacob's well. Samaritans were a product of the Assyrian exile and were not fully Jewish. They were half breeds and were totally disregarded by the nation of Israel. In fact, the Jews wouldn't even talk to the Samaritans. But, the feeling was mutual, because the Samaritans hated the Jewish people too. The two groups maintained an intense hatred toward one another.

> *The woman from Shomron* [Samaria] *said to him*
> [Yeshua], *"How is it that you, a Jew, ask for water*
> *from me, a woman of Shomron?" (For Jews don't*
> *associate with people from Shomron.)*
>
> *Yeshua answered her, "if you knew God's gift, that*
> *is, who it is saying to you, 'Give me a drink of water,'*
> *then you would have asked him; and he would have*
> *given you living water."* (John 4:9-10)

Yeshua spoke to this Samaritan woman, and they discussed the living water and their worship, but Yeshua in no way approved the woman's worship. In fact, He said, *You people don't know what you are worshipping; we worship what we do know, because salvation comes from the Jews* (John 4:22). The Samaritan worship wasn't authorized or sanctioned by God; they had their own form of worship. Yeshua was absolutely condemning the Samaritan mode of worship when He said they didn't even know what they were worshipping. He told her there was only one way. He said *we worship*, because God gave instructions on worship to the Jewish people. God appointed the Jewish people to be His messengers. It was to them that He gave the Scriptures. So, the Messiah came to this woman and told her *salvation comes from the Jews.* The ultimate descendant of Israel, the Messiah of Israel, Yeshua Himself, would be the ultimate smoking fire pot and the ultimate flaming torch.

Messiah in Isaiah

If we open the book of Isaiah, we see this salvation that God has provided. Isaiah is the prophet of prophets. *Yesha'yahu,* *Isaiah,* means "salvation," and salvation is referred to more in that book than in all of the other prophetic books combined – major, minor, and post-exilic included. Isaiah mentions the word *salvation* twenty-four times, which is more than all the other prophetic books in the Bible combined.

There are sixty-six books in the Bible and sixty-six chapters in Isaiah. The first thirty-nine chapters in Isaiah talk about a sin problem, and the first thirty-nine books of the Bible, the Old Testament, talk about a sin problem. The next twenty-seven chapters in Isaiah and the remaining twenty-seven books of the Bible, the New Testament, talk about the solution to that sin problem.

In Isaiah 42:1, God said, *Here is my servant, whom I support, my chosen one, in whom I take pleasure.* The word *servant,* when used in the Old Testament, means one of three things. One, *servant* can indicate the entire nation of Israel. Two, *servant* can also be used to refer to the godly remnant of Israel, or three, *servant* can refer to Messiah. In order to know which definition Isaiah is referring to, we must read it in context with the surrounding verses.

Here is my servant, whom I support, my chosen one, in whom I take pleasure. I have put my Spirit on him; he will bring justice to the Goyim [nations]. *He will not cry or shout; no one will hear his voice in the streets. He will not snap off a broken reed or snuff out a smoldering wick. He will bring forth justice according to truth; he will not weaken or be crushed until he has established justice on the earth, and the coastlands wait for his Torah* [law]. (Isaiah 42:1-4)

So, who is this servant? In Isaiah 53:11, it says, *After this ordeal, he will see satisfaction. "By his knowing [pain and sacrifice], my righteous servant makes many righteous; it is for their sins that he suffers."* The only place in the Bible that this term *righteous servant* is spoken of is in this place, so it's referring to either Messiah or Israel. But if Israel was perfectly righteous, she wouldn't have been exiled to Babylon.

In Isaiah 50:6, Adonai says, *I offered my back to those who struck me, my cheeks to those who plucked out my beard.* By considering these other verses in Isaiah, chapter 42 must be speaking about Messiah. It says, *He will not snap*

> And if a person has a smoldering wick of faith, He won't quench it. That's a good God.

off a broken reed. In other words, He will not crush true repentance. If a person truly repents and says, "I'm sorry, I don't want this way of life, I want to follow You," He will not crush even that little bit of repentance. And if a person has a *smoldering wick* of faith, He won't quench it. That's a good God. We aren't in a position to decide whether a person is truly repentant or not; we can leave that to God. He says He will not weaken or be crushed until He has established justice on the earth. According to Isaiah, the Messiah will not fail or be discouraged until He establishes His righteous kingdom.

I love when he says, *and the coastlands wait for his Torah.* The land shall come under the Torah? Yes, the Torah of God; this is referring to His ways, His teaching, and His heart.. God's heart would care for the poor and the widow. He would keep the land in the family. He wouldn't glean the crops to the corners. No matter how hard we may try to obey the Torah, nobody does it perfectly. This doesn't mean we shouldn't aim to do as much as we can, but there will be a time when He establishes His kingdom and our obedience will be perfect.

Continuing in Isaiah 42 with the flaming-torch aspect of Yeshua, we read:

Thus says God, ADONAI, who created the heavens and spread them out, who stretched out the earth and all that grows from it, who gives breath to the people on it and spirit to those who walk on it: "I, ADONAI, called you righteously, I took hold of you by the hand, I shaped you and made you a covenant for the people, to be a light for the Goyim [nations], *so that you can open blind eyes, free the prisoners from confinement, those living in darkness from the dungeon.* (Isaiah 42:5-7)

God the mighty Creator is addressing Yeshua and telling Him what He will accomplish through Him. Why do you think Yeshua made His grandiose statement in John 8:12, right after Sukkot, the Feast of Tabernacles? They had been praying for Messiah to come. They were praying for the waters of salvation, the living waters, *Mayim Chayim. Then you will joyfully draw water from the springs of salvation* (Isaiah 12:3). On Sukkot, they prayed that the Lord would come and tabernacle among them. In the midst of this, they were pouring water and praying for the living waters to come. The next day, they lit giant menorahs all around, so all of Jerusalem would be lit up as they prayed for the Light of the World to come. In the midst of this ceremony, *Yeshua spoke to them again: "I am the light of the world; whoever follows me will never walk in darkness but will have the light which gives life"* (John 8:12).

Yeshua was telling them, "I'm here!" But it wasn't enough to just recognize the Light. They needed to walk in the Light.

The profession that He is the Light isn't enough. Even the Devil believes that. *You believe that "God is one"? Good for you! The demons believe it too – the thought makes them shudder with fear!* (James 2:19). Yeshua said that whoever followed Him would never walk in darkness but have the Light that gives life. Yeshua is the deliverer. Not only was He the Light of the World, but He was also the smoking fire pot.

> Yeshua said that whoever followed Him would never walk in darkness but have the Light that gives life.

Look at Isaiah 53:3-5 to understand suffering in regards to the smoking fire pot:

> *People despised and avoided him, a man of pains, well acquainted with illness. Like someone from whom people turn their faces, he was despised; we did not value him. In fact, it was our diseases he bore, our pains from which he suffered; yet we regarded him as punished, stricken and afflicted by God. But he was wounded because of our crimes, crushed because of our sins; the disciplining that makes us whole fell on him, and by his bruises we are healed.*

The people despised Him, and they avoided Him. He wasn't some rock star with fans crowding around Him. He was the Man of Sorrows. If you're walking with the Lord and people don't despise and avoid you, you're probably not walking the right walk. Not everybody will be persecuted to the point of death, but you'll have those who despise you. He wasn't a politician; there was nothing political about Him. He wasn't trying to be politically incorrect, but when you're walking in truth, you will be politically incorrect.

He was a man of pains, and He wept as He looked at the people. They were sheep without a shepherd, so He sat down to teach them. This Man of Sorrows, this man of pains, was well acquainted with illness. He bore our diseases, suffered our pains, and was punished for us. Some people believe that when someone gets sick or is afflicted, it must be from some secret sin. This is not always true, for some of the greatest men and women of God suffered severely, and it had nothing to do with their walk. He was wounded because of our crimes and crushed for our sins. The disciplining, the rod that makes us whole, fell on Him, and *by His bruises we are healed.*

> Every human being is looking for Yeshua, but they're looking in the wrong places and will never be satisfied until they find Him.

Yeshua announced this to His disciples: *Then, taking the Twelve, Yeshua said to them, "We are now going up to Yerushalayim* [Jerusalem], *where everything written through the prophets about the Son of Man will come true. For he will be handed over* (Luke 18:31-32). Remember, there was no New Testament, but these people were very proficient in the Old Testament and the prophecies. Everybody was looking for Messiah, and many still are. Deep down, everyone is looking for Messiah. *He has made everything suited to its time; also, he has given human beings an awareness of eternity; but in such a way that they can't fully comprehend, from beginning to end, the things God does* (Ecclesiastes 3:11). Every human being is looking for that eternity; they're looking for love. Everyone is looking to be loved and affirmed and cared for, and they want security and protection. Every human being is looking for Yeshua, but they're looking in the wrong places and will never be satisfied until they find Him.

So, just like the prophets had said, Yeshua went on to say, *"For he will be handed over to the Goyim* [nations] *and be ridiculed, insulted and spat upon. Then, after they have beaten him, they will kill him. But on the third day he will rise"* (Luke 18:32-33). He foretold exactly what would happen to Him. He was handed over to the Romans because the Jews didn't have the authority in their laws to crucify anyone. They couldn't do it. The Romans, however, crucified people on a regular basis. Why was He handed over to the Gentiles? Well, God used the Gentiles to punish Israel for their sin, so Yeshua had to be handed over to the Gentiles to pay for their sin. He was handed over to them, and they took Him to their courts where He was ridiculed, insulted, spit on, beaten, and then killed – just like He said. But on the third day, He said He would rise. However, the disciples didn't understand this; they couldn't figure out how this worked into God's plan.

Have you ever asked God, "God, if you're so loving, why am I going through all this stuff?" When I was in my thirties, I didn't focus on eternal life. People told me about eternal life, but I had perfect health and lived near the beach in a small house with my wife. She had perfect health, and we had one child with another on the way. Everything was great. I didn't need to focus on eternal life. I had a relationship with God, and life was too good to be true. If you had asked me if I wanted Yeshua to come back, I probably would have said yes, but I didn't want too much to change.

Then my body started to fall apart, and now I'm looking forward to a new body. I've learned that it doesn't make you less of a believer, and it doesn't make God love you less when you struggle. In all fairness, these struggles help us focus on eternal life. Personally, I need a new body, and some people need to see their dearly departed loved ones again. If you take that hope away, we have nothing. I'm living for that day when

Yeshua says, "Well done." I'm also look-

In all fairness, these struggles help us focus on eternal life.

ing forward to the time when everything around me is perfect. I want to experience that bliss like in the garden of Eden. I know when we're young, we

want to enjoy something in this life now, and we should, but we need to keep God in the center of it all. Our perfect lives don't stay perfect forever, so we need to be prepared and keep our eyes on the Lord.

Yeshua's disciples couldn't understand either. How did this all fit in God's plan? Yeshua Himself had to face flogging and crucifixion. Even Yeshua, the God-Man, the One who was very confident of His resurrection, very confident of His ascension, and very confident of being back with His Father said, *"Father, if you are willing, take this cup away from me; still, let not my will but yours be done"* (Luke 22:42). So, if He could tell His Father His load was too heavy, then we can too.

We do walk by faith, but some people's faith-walk is more difficult than others' faith-walk. Consider Job and his walk of faith as he lost everything. When Horatio Spafford lost his four daughters, he wrote the hymn "It Is Well With My Soul." Our friends in Kenya and India face persecution daily. It's hard to trust Him, but what else do we have? We have hope. In this life, there is persecution, but what's waiting for us on the other side is where our hope is, and that's what we have faith in. *Trusting is being confident of what we hope for, convinced about things we do not see* (Hebrews 11:1).

So, this fulfillment of prophecy wasn't a horrible accident. It was prophesied; it was foretold. Nobody took His life – not the Romans, not the Jews, not even your sins. He said nobody took His life; He laid it down; He gave it up. *No one takes it away from me; on the contrary, I lay it down of my own free will* (John 10:18). It was a burnt offering, a free-will offering. He gave His life to show us two things. First, we have great redemptive value; we are very special to Him. Every one of us has some spiritual gifting that God placed in us. The other thing He showed us is that sin really messes things up, and it hurts people.

God Himself had made the covenantal promises with Abraham and Israel, but the disciples didn't really understand all Yeshua was talking about. Maybe sometimes we don't understand either, but *we live by trust, not by what we see.* By living in this faith here and now, we can endeavor to live a life for God.

Chapter 3

An Acceptable Offering

Importance of Leviticus

As we think about eternal life and living for God, we need to go back to Leviticus. Why? Let me quote Andrew Bonar, a theologian and minister in the Free Church of Scotland in the 1800s. He had an extreme love for Israel and the Jewish people. When Bonar was talking about Leviticus, he said, "There is no book in the whole compass of that inspired volume which the Holy Spirit has given us that contains more of the very words of God than Leviticus. It is God that is the direct speaker in almost every page. His gracious words are recorded in the form in which they were spoken. This consideration cannot fail to send us to the study of it with singular interest and attention."[6] (Short disclaimer: When I quote a person, I'm not saying that

---

6   Andrew Bonar, *A Commentary on the Book of Leviticus* (New York: Robert Carter & Brothers, 1851), 1.

I adhere to all of their theology. I'm only drawing attention to and agreeing with the quote.)

People claim to want to hear God speak to them, and here we have a book where God is speaking directly on almost every page. This fact should cause us to read and study this book with particular interest and care. But John Nelson Darby once warned of the dire results if believers grew bored with holiness. Holiness is the main theme of Leviticus, and this book certainly is the hardest one for many Christians to read.[7]

Twenty of the twenty-seven chapters in Leviticus and thirty-five of the paragraphs start with *ADONAI spoke to Moshe* [Moses]. Ninety-nine percent of the book is the Lord speaking, not Moses going into the tent of meeting and coming out and saying, "Thus says the Lord." In Leviticus, God is speaking. That's how potent this book is. If we think this is just an ancient Jewish sacrificial rules and regulations manual to maintain holiness in everyday life, then we miss the point of the book. God wants Christians to be holy too. Both in the Old Testament and in the New Testament, God says, *be holy, for I am holy* (Leviticus 11:44; 1 Peter 1:16). There's just one problem. Man, by nature and practice, is unholy even when he strives to be holy. There's a great chasm that needs to be bridged.

To love and appreciate Leviticus, we need to understand how the sacrifices in this book point to the ultimate sacrifice; they point to Yeshua. We also need to understand how that knowledge affects how we live now. There's no need to approach this book as some vast mystery because God wants us to understand it. We would do well to heed the words of E. F. Schumacher: "Any intelligent fool can make things bigger,

---

7   William MacDonald, *Believer's Bible Commentary* (Nashville, TN: Thomas Nelson Publishers, Inc., 1995), 135.

more complex, and more violent. It takes a touch of genius – and a lot of courage – to move in the opposite direction."[8] Leviticus doesn't need to be complicated and complex. When we make it that intellectual, we're only lifting ourselves up and putting ourselves on a podium above other people.

With that in mind, we'll simplify this book instead of portraying it as an enigma of the mystery behind the veil. Leviticus chapters 1 through 7 show us five offerings. First is the burnt offering. Then we see the grain offering, which is the same as the meal offering in some Bible versions. Next is the peace offering, which is sometimes called the fellowship offering in some versions. The last two are the sin offering and the guilt offering. Five offerings: burnt, grain, peace, sin, and guilt.

> Our offering is a sacrifice, and it comes in many forms. It's not just money, but also time, talents, and treasures.

We've already seen what *offering* means, but if we look at the New Testament, we see that Yeshua told His followers not to treat their offering as *corban*. He said, *"You have made a fine art of departing from God's command in order to keep your tradition! . . . Thus, with your tradition which you had handed down to you, you nullify the Word of God!"* (Mark 7:9, 13). This is in the context of where Yeshua reminded them to honor their fathers and mothers.

Our offering is a sacrifice, and it comes in many forms. It's not just money, but also time, talents, and treasures. An offering is an act of love, so the greater the offering, the greater the love. Remember, the root word means to come near or to join. God set this sacrificial system up so we could draw near to

---

8   Ernst Friedrich Schumacher, "Small is Beautiful," *The Radical Humanist*, Vol. 37, No. 5 (August 1973), 22.

Him, because that's His heart's desire. It's not an afterthought. He really wants to be close to us, like loving parents want their children to be close to them.

Leviticus depicts these five offerings, five being the number in Gematria that signifies grace. Gematria is biblical numerology, not psychic numerology, but a method of interpreting the Hebrew Scriptures by computing the numerical value of words. In this system, *five* stands for grace.

The first five books of the Bible are the books of Moses or the Torah. They're also called the Pentateuch. Five spices comprise the anointing oil in Exodus: myrrh, cinnamon, cane, cassia, and olive oil. *Take the best spices – 500 shekels of myrrh [12 1/2 pounds], half this amount (250 shekels) of aromatic cinnamon [6 1/4 pounds], 250 shekels of aromatic cane, 500 shekels of cassia (use the sanctuary standard), and one gallon of olive oil* (Exodus 30:23-24).

The first three offerings were totally voluntary, and the next two were compulsory. The sin and the guilt offerings were the required sacrifices.

Daniel described five kingdoms to King Nebuchadnezzar, the last of which was to be the everlasting kingdom. *In the days of those kings the God of heaven will establish a kingdom that will never be destroyed, and that kingdom will not pass into the hands of another people. It will break to pieces and consume all those kingdoms; but it, itself, will stand forever* (Daniel 2:44). This fifth kingdom is God's kingdom, promised through His grace to the Jewish people.

To have five offerings was also significant, particularly when we remember that the offering was God's way of allowing man to approach Him or join with Him. It was through His grace that He made such a provision. The first three offerings were totally voluntary, and the next two were compulsory. The sin and the guilt offerings were the required sacrifices.

Burnt Offering

Leviticus speaks of the offerings themselves with all the detail – what they are, the duties of the offeror, the duties and responsibilities of the priest, and how the offering was distributed. They aren't complex, but we can't expect to read through them quickly and understand them. We need to take our time to fully comprehend.

Looking at the instructions for the burnt offering, we read, *If his offering is a burnt offering from the herd, he must offer a male without defect. He is to bring it to the entrance of the tent of meeting, so that it can be accepted by* ADONAI (Leviticus 1:3).

The entrance to the tent of meeting isn't actually the entrance to the whole tent. When the Bible speaks about the tent of meeting, the sanctuary, it's referring to the inner sanctuary, which is comprised of the Holy Place and the Holy of Holies. The Holy of Holies contained the ark of the covenant, and the Holy Place contained the bread of the presence, the menorah, and the altar of incense. Before they entered the sanctuary, they walked into the outer courtyard of the tent with the brazen altar and the brazen laver. That was where the sacrifices were made. Sacrifices weren't offered every day, except for the eternal sacrifice. They didn't have to travel to Jerusalem every time they sinned. They offered their sacrifices during the high holy days and the other holidays.

The people came and made these sacrifices at different times of the year to encapsulate their hearts, but they could still repent in their hearts at any time wherever they were. We still have to do that as new-covenant believers. They brought these sacrifices, so they could be accepted by Adonai. *It is an offering made by fire, a fragrant aroma for ADONAI* (Leviticus 1:9).

This sacrifice was *without defect*. In the Hebrew language, the word *tamim* means "complete, whole, and innocent." This offering was voluntary, but they had to give it in its entirety. Yeshua gave Himself in His entirety as a voluntary act. In the gospel of John, Yeshua said, *No one takes it away from me; on the contrary, I lay it down of my own free will* (John 10:18). First, we need to realize that Yeshua died in obedience to His Father. Secondly, nobody took His life; He laid it down as a voluntary act. The burnt offering speaks of His innocence and His voluntary action – a picture of Messiah, without spot, before God. He was totally and completely consumed in the fires of divine judgment, even though He was completely innocent for thirty-three years. This is incomprehensible and so difficult for us to wrap our minds around, as we tend to struggle with being innocent for just thirty-three minutes.

In the New Testament, we see Peter, a nice Jewish boy who was a direct disciple of Yeshua, who wrote a letter to areas which are now Turkey. He wrote about the suffering, because every first-century believer suffered. It was standard operating procedure – all believers in Yeshua were persecuted, beaten, imprisoned, and even killed. That went without saying, but it's very different today. Not all believers are being persecuted at the moment, but that could change, because to whom much is given, much is required. *From him who has been given much, much will be demanded — from someone to whom people entrust much, they ask still more* (Luke 12:48). At some point, we might experience first-century persecution, and in some countries around the world today, believers already experience daily persecution. It's just not here yet.

Peter said, *You should be aware that the ransom paid to free you from the worthless way of life which your fathers passed on to you did not consist of anything perishable like silver or gold* (1 Peter 1:18). Peter was telling them that the ransom was priceless, worth more than tens of thousands of talents of gold. Today, Christians have heard for so long about the price Jesus paid that it has become commonplace, and its significance lost on us.

> There's not a big division or chasm between the Old and the New – it's God's Word – period.

When we read in the Bible that Jesus was flogged, or Jesus was crucified, what does that mean to us? His suffering didn't consist of anything perishable like silver or gold. *On the contrary, it was the costly bloody sacrificial death of the Messiah, as of a lamb without defect or spot* (1 Peter 1:19). Peter was speaking of Yeshua as the burnt offering. We see that the writings of the New Testament are exactly like the Old Testament here because it's the Word of God. There's not a big division or chasm between the Old and the New – it's God's Word – period.

Grain Offering

The grain offering appears in the second chapter of Leviticus, which says, *Anyone who brings a grain offering to ADONAI is to make his offering of fine flour; he is to pour olive oil on it and put frankincense on it . . . No grain offering that you bring to ADONAI is to be made with leaven, because you are not to cause any leaven or honey to go up in smoke as an offering made by fire to ADONAI* (Leviticus 2:1, 11).

I want to look at this symbolically, but I don't want to encourage the tendency to spiritualize things that shouldn't be spiritualized or make them into what they're not. To avoid this kind of spiritualization, we must take the illustration and make sure it's consistent throughout the Scriptures. We can't just take something and make a theology out of one sentence, but when the Bible speaks of fine flour, it's speaking of something untainted. We know that Yeshua's life was morally perfect; He was tempted but didn't sin. When He was tired, he had to sleep. That's why He was sleeping in the boat. When He was hungry, He said He was hungry and wanted to eat.

When God speaks about olive oil, it's always consistent – olive oil always refers to the Holy Spirit. Yeshua was full of the Holy Spirit. In fact, John recorded that He received the Spirit without measure: *The one whom God sent speaks God's words. For God does not give him the Spirit in limited degree* (John 3:34). That means the Spirit kept pouring in, and there was no time in His tabernacle when the Spirit's presence was lacking.

Why was Yeshua fragrant? He was totally and completely obedient.

Frankincense was put on the fine flour and always refers to a fragrant offering to God. Why was Yeshua fragrant? He was totally and completely obedient. The flour had no leaven, because leaven always speaks of sin, and He was untainted by evil. Not only did He defeat Satan on the cross, but He also defeated Satan in the wilderness at the start of His ministry. He told Satan he had no hold on Him and showed him that he couldn't touch Him, and He wouldn't give in (Matthew 4:1-11).

This grain offering speaks of Yeshua. Look at Hebrews, which is obviously written to Jewish believers, and the main theme is that the sacrificial system is no more because the great High Priest has come. The writer of Hebrews said, *For we do not have a cohen gadol* [high priest] *unable to empathize with our weaknesses; since in every respect he was tempted just as we are, the only difference being that he did not sin* (Hebrews 4:15). All of us have weaknesses, and just as we are tempted, He was tempted in every way. The only difference – He did not sin. That's a huge difference. Yeshua came down to earth to live this out for us, and when He left, He sent the Holy Spirit to help give us the ability to say no to Satan.

> *If your offering is a grain offering cooked on a griddle, it is to consist of unleavened fine flour mixed with olive oil . . . The cohen* [priest] *is to cause the reminder portion of it, its grits and olive oil, with all its frankincense, to go up in smoke; it is an offering made by fire for ADONAI.* (Leviticus 2:5, 16)

The Jewish people have given us great things in the physical world. We can thank them for Novocain when we visit the dentist. Alfred Einhorn, a Jewish German chemist, developed procaine, which was patented as Novocain.[9] The Jews' list of contributions in biomedicine is quite extensive, saving innumerable lives through their intelligence and hard work. They discovered the ABO blood groups and developed Coumadin, cardiac defibrillators, and external pacemakers and monitors.[10] Henry Heimlich, son of Jewish parents Philip and Mary Heimlich, developed the Heimlich maneuver, which has saved the lives of many choking victims.[11]

But more significant than these physical inventions and advances in medicine is their legacy in the spiritual realm. The Jewish people gave us monotheism, the belief that there is only one God, *"Sh'ma, Yisra'el! ADONAI Eloheinu, ADONAI echad*

---

9   *en.wikipedia.org/wiki/Alfred_Einhorn.*
10   *www.jinfo.org/Biomedical_Research.html.*
11   *en.wikipedia.org/wiki/Henry_Heimlich.*

[Hear, Isra'el! ADONAI our God, ADONAI is one] (Deuteronomy 6:4). They preserved their oracles and gave us the Bible. *In the first place, the Jews were entrusted with the very words of God* (Romans 3:2). Out of Yeshua's own mouth, He said the Jews gave us Messiah, *because salvation comes from the Jews* (John 4:22).

An interesting part of these couple of verses in Leviticus 2 is where it says they cook the grain offering on the griddle, and the fine flour turns into grits. So, this Jew from New York City (me) can come down here to the South (Georgia) and say, "The Jewish people invented grits." We even camped for forty years in the wilderness before folks today decided they loved camping around their fire pits. We Jews had the fire burning 24/7, and it never went out (Leviticus 6:12-13).

But seriously, we need to look at this word *grits*, because it means more than Southern grits with gravy. In Hebrew, it means "a crushing." The great prophecy about the Messiah says, *But he was wounded because of our crimes, crushed because of our sins* (Isaiah 53:5). Crushed! In the Hebrew that means "completely shattered." When crystal falls and hits stone, it shatters into a million pieces. That's what Messiah was – shattered. Completely shattered, as shown in the grain offering.

Peace Offering

Leviticus 3 gives us the next offering. Chapter 1 was the burnt offering, and chapter 2 was the grain offering. Now we see the peace offering: *If his offering is a sacrifice of peace offerings, then, if he offers before ADONAI an animal from the herd, then, no matter whether it is male or female, it must be without defect* (Leviticus 3:1). This peace offering is still one of the voluntary offerings, and this verse tells us that if we want to draw close to God, we need to give Him our best. How often do we take

our worn-out clothes to the rescue mission? Or maybe a broken fan? This isn't the place to get rid of our junk. We need to
give God our best.

> He is to lay his hand on the head of his offering
> and slaughter it at the entrance to the tent of meet-
> ing; and the sons of Aharon [Aaron], the cohanim
> [priests], are to splash the blood against all sides of
> the altar . . . The cohen [priest] will make them go
> up in smoke on the altar; it is food, an offering made
> by fire to be a fragrant aroma; all the fat belongs to
> ADONAI. It is to be a permanent regulation through
> all your generations wherever you live that you will
> eat neither fat nor blood. (Leviticus 3:2, 16-17)

Let's backtrack a bit for a better understanding. Levi was one of
the twelve sons of Jacob, and the tribe of Levi was responsible
for all the work in the tabernacle: *Give the L'vi'im [Levites]
charge over the tabernacle of the tes-
timony, its equipment and everything* **This isn't the place to get**
else connected with it. They are to carry **rid of our junk. We need**
the tabernacle and all its equipment, **to give God our best.**
*serve in it and set up their camp around
it. When the tabernacle is to be moved onward, it is the L'vi'im
who are to take it down and set it up in the new location; anyone
else who involves himself is to be put to death* (Numbers 1:50-
51). Aaron was a Levite; he and his descendants were chosen
to be the priests of the tabernacle; they were the Cohanim. *You
are to summon your brother Aharon and his sons to come from
among the people of Isra'el to you, so that they can serve me as
cohanim [priests] – Aharon and his sons Nadav, Avihu, El'azar*

and Itamar (Exodus 28:1). The Levites were responsible for the putting up, taking down, and cleaning of the tabernacle, but the Cohanim were the descendants of Aaron, the ones who made the sacrifices.

If we look at the word *fat*, we know it refers to the oily, greasy substance of human or animal physiology, but it also means choicest or finest. The fat here, in regard to Yeshua, represents the very best part of the animal. It was given to the Lord as one worthy of honor, but the priest didn't take it, and the offeror didn't take it. It was reserved for the Lord – give the Lord the best. Yeshua was God's best. He couldn't give anything better than a piece of Himself in human form. God gave His best for earth's worst.

> The offering became a stench to His nostrils because the people's hearts weren't in the offerings.

The offering became a stench to His nostrils because the people's hearts weren't in the offerings. Do you remember J. Hudson Taylor? He was the greatest evangelist since the apostle Paul, and he had such a heart for the Chinese people that he went there in 1853 and started the China Inland Mission. They wouldn't listen to him and called him the black devil, because he wore a long black coat. So he adopted the native Chinese clothes and grew a long pigtail. He shaved his hair and learned their language. After that, the Chinese began to realize that he wasn't the black devil and maybe he really cared. He had three hundred mission stations and eighteen thousand converts. James Hudson Taylor gave his best.[12]

I consider Leviticus 17:11 the quintessential verse in the

12   Christian History Magazine Editorial Staff, Mark Galli, *131 Christians Everyone Should Know* (Nashville, TN: Holman Reference, 2000), 251-253: *www.christianitytoday.com/history/people/missionaries/hudson-taylor.html.*

book of Leviticus; it says, *For the life of a creature is in the blood, and I have given it to you on the altar to make atonement for yourselves; for it is the blood that makes atonement because of the life.* God says He has given the blood for them, but if you ask a Jew what they do today for atonement, they'll say, "What do you mean? There's no temple." There's a reason there's no temple – the sacrificial system is no longer necessary; however, there will be a temple when Yeshua returns.

So the blood was reserved for atonement. Consider the word *blood*; the Hebrew word *dam* means "blood or death." This definition tells us that when the Jews gave a sacrifice, they couldn't just draw blood. They had to bleed the animal until it died. This was how they made atonement. Likewise, Yeshua couldn't just bleed; He had to die. Therefore, in the Messiah, the sinner and God meet in peace because the blood reconciles us.

We can see this connection in Colossians when Paul wrote his letter to this small congregation. God is speaking to the people of Colossae here, and He's speaking about the head of the body of believers, which is none other than Yeshua Himself. He says, *and through his Son to reconcile to himself all things, whether on earth or in heaven, making peace through him, through having his Son shed his blood by being executed on a stake* (Colossians 1:20).

This makes me think of the cherubim, the two angels who were on the mercy seat, whose wings touched as they were looking down. It's like the cherubim waited all year to see the blood of the lamb on the mercy seat. They waited for the Day of Atonement when the high priest came in and put the blood on the mercy seat seven times. Then they'd be satisfied. But I see that God waited even longer to see Yeshua's blood on the mercy seat. In fact, Yeshua is the mercy seat, and His slab in the tomb was the ark; He covered it, because He is our seat of mercy.

But the word *blood* has another root, which means "guilt of blood" or "guilty of blood." This is evident when Zipporah circumcised her son. She called Moses a bridegroom of blood and threw the foreskin at him, because he was not being obedient and was bringing the blood of judgment on the family. *At a lodging-place on the way, ADONAI met Moshe [Moses] and would have killed him, had not Tzipporah taken a flintstone and cut off the foreskin of her son. She threw it at his feet, saying, "What a bloody bridegroom you are for me!" But then, God let Moshe be. She added, "A bloody bridegroom because of the circumcision!"* (Exodus 4:24-26). This root means "guilty of murder."

This raises a question: do you want to accept Yeshua's sacrifice, or do you want to be responsible for it? Sometimes, Christians only teach that He died for our sins, but it's bigger than that, because some people think they're pretty good. They can recite a long list of what they've done: worked at an AIDS clinic, given money to the cancer society, raised a family, never committed adultery, etc. They think their good outweighs their bad. If that's true, then why do we carry around so much guilt? Yeshua's sacrifice not only covers our sin, but it removes the guilt of our sin. So either we receive His sacrifice or we will be responsible for it.

In Leviticus 3, God gives instructions for the peace offering three times – once for the offering from the herd, once for the offering from the flock, and once for the offering of a goat (Leviticus 3:1, 6, 12). In each of these, the offeror brought the animal to the altar, laid his hand on it, and killed it. Then the priest sprinkled the blood on the altar, cut up the animal, took his portion, gave the offeror his portion, and burned God's portion as a fragrant aroma. God, the priest, and the man all shared the same meal, picturing a peaceful fellowship.

In this sacrifice the Messiah played all three parts: He is the offeror, because He brought the sacrifice to the altar and laid it down. He is the priest, because He serves mankind as the one Mediator and most importantly, He is the offering, because He was the sacrifice.

Sin Offering

The sin offering is the first of the compulsory offerings. In Leviticus 4, God begins by saying, *"Tell the people of Isra'el: 'If anyone sins inadvertently.'"* What does He mean by *inadvertent*? Many sins are inadvertent in that they are mistakes. But we sin purposely when we walk in sin, knowing it's wrong. Do we think cheating on our taxes is okay? Is it okay for us to cheat the government when we believe it cheats us? Two wrongs don't make a right. In fact, one wrong plus one wrong equals two wrongs, every day of the week.

> God, the priest, and the man all shared the same meal, picturing a peaceful fellowship.

So God says, *Tell the people of Isra'el: 'If anyone sins inadvertently against any of the mitzvot* [commandments] *of ADONAI concerning things which should not be done, if he does any one of them, then, if it is the anointed cohen* [priest] *who sinned and thus brought guilt on the people, he is to offer ADONAI a young bull without defect as a sin offering for the sin he committed . . . The cohen is to dip his finger in the blood and sprinkle some of the blood seven times in the presence of ADONAI in front of the curtain of the sanctuary . . . thus the cohen will make atonement for him in regard to his sin, and he will be forgiven* (Leviticus 4:1-3, 6, 26).

The word *forgiven* means "to be pardoned." In legal terminology *pardon* means "to release from the penalty of offense, an acquittal." The number seven speaks of spiritual perfection and completeness and is tied closely to God's seven-day creation week with God's Sabbath being the seventh day. The book of Revelation describes seven churches, seven angels, seven seals, seven trumpets, and seven thunders. Between Genesis and Revelation, the number seven continues to appear.

As part of the sin offering, the priest dipped his finger in the blood and sprinkled some of it seven times in front of the sanctuary. This symbolically pointed

We get to share in God's righteousness.

to Messiah who was made sin for us, although He Himself never succumbed to sin. The innocent victim's death was regarded symbolically as the sinner's death; therefore, they always laid hands on the animal to show they were transferring their sin to the animal.

God made this sinless man be a sin offering on our behalf, so that in union with him we might fully share in God's righteousness (2 Corinthians 5:21). Today, people can commit crimes, but sometimes get off on a technicality. The judge will declare that the criminal can go free, but what we receive is way bigger than a technicality. We get to share in *God's righteousness*. As we saw earlier, God provided an innocent victim to die as a substitute for another. *By his knowing [pain and sacrifice], my righteous servant makes many righteous; it is for their sins that he suffers* (Isaiah 53:11). An innocent little lamb went to the slaughter and didn't even open its mouth. The apostle Paul explained to the Corinthians that the innocent lamb is our Messiah when he said, *For our Pesach* [Passover] *lamb, the Messiah, has been sacrificed* (1 Corinthians 5:7).

Guilt Offering

Two verses in Leviticus 5 speak of the guilt offering. *If anyone acts improperly and inadvertently sins in regard to the holy things of* ADONAI, *he is to bring as his guilt offering for* ADONAI *a ram without defect from the flock or its equivalent in silver shekels (using the sanctuary shekel as the standard), according to your appraisal of its value; it is a guilt offering . . . It is a guilt offering – he is certainly guilty before* ADONAI (Leviticus 5:15, 19). When we feel guilty, it's a good thing, because the guilt will bring on repentance. First, we experience guilt, then we confess, which brings us to the door of repentance. True repentance brings us through the door in order to connect or reconnect with God. There's nothing wrong with guilt handled this way. *Pain handled in God's way produces a turning from sin to God which leads to salvation, and there is nothing to regret in that!* (2 Corinthians 7:10).

Look at the word *guilt*. The Hebrew word is *asham* and it means "an offense, a trespass, a fault," but it also means "compensation." In other words, somebody has to pay.

Continuing in Leviticus 5, verse 21 says, *If someone sins and acts perversely against* ADONAI *by dealing falsely with his neighbor.* Some of us are very guilty here. When someone goes through a divorce, and their house is worth $300,000, we're tempted to scoop it up for $100,000. I'm telling you, if we do that, we're wrong. Conducting business with people as long as we use fair weights and measures is appropriate. Taking advantage of people when they are down and out is not good, and it is not God's way. Praying for them as we rob them blind isn't right either. God says, *If someone sins and acts perversely against ADONAI by dealing falsely with his neighbor in regard to a deposit or security entrusted to him, by stealing from him, by extorting him, or by dealing falsely in regard to a lost object he has found* (Leviticus 5:21-22). When I started to read my Bible, I realized that if I found something that someone had lost, I had to find the person who lost it. Sometimes I thought I'd be better off just leaving it where I found it instead of picking it up. Who knows? The owner might come back. It's not finders keepers, losers weepers. That's not God's way.

He goes on to say, *or by swearing to a lie – if a person commits any of these sins, then, if he sinned and is guilty, he is to restore whatever it was he stole or obtained by extortion, or whatever was deposited with him, or the lost object which he found, or anything about which he has sworn falsely* (Leviticus 5:22-24). If we rob someone, we can't just say, "I'm sorry." Restore whatever it was. Even if the person forgives us, restore it anyway. It may take many years, but make an effort to restore and repay. If we can't pay it back, maybe we can work it off: wash a car, mow a lawn, or clean a house. The Bible tells us that those of us who are spiritual need to restore. If we aren't in the restoration business, we're not in the spiritual business.

If we aren't in the restoration business, we're not in the spiritual business.

Reading further in chapter 5, He says, *He is to restore it in full plus an additional one-fifth; he must return it to the person who owns it, on the day when he presents his guilt offering. He is to bring as his guilt offering to ADONAI a ram without defect from the flock, or its equivalent according to your appraisal, to the cohen* [priest]; *it is a guilt offering. Thus the cohen will make atonement for him before ADONAI, and he will be forgiven in regard to whatever it was he did that made him guilty* (Leviticus 5:24-26). He will be forgiven. Praise God. He doesn't have to die in his sin because God is a good God – He's a loving God. He's a wonderful God who makes a way for us.

Look at the word *restore*. It means "to make whole, to make restitution, to compensate." The person bringing a guilt offering sought to make amends for some action of his that caused loss or damage to God or someone else, and he would be atoned. The word for *atone* is *kaphar* in Hebrew, which means "to cover." The guilt would be covered, and the person would be reconciled. If the offended person says not to worry about it, that's his prerogative, and he's entitled to be full of grace, but as the sinner, we can't expect that grace. That would be taking advantage of grace.

Paul tells us in the book of Romans that *God put Yeshua forward as the kapparah* [atonement] *for sin through his faithfulness in respect to his bloody sacrificial death* (Romans 3:25). God presented His Son as our *kippur*, our atonement for sin in a bloody sacrificial execution. This was not a benign sacrifice. It was dirty. Isaiah 53:10 says it *pleased* God to crush Him, to shatter Him, to smash Him to pieces. How can that be? That doesn't sound right. How could God be pleased to *crush* His Son? He didn't even do anything wrong. Those are strong words, strong terminology, to express the completeness of the sacrifice. Through sin, God and man were separated; God was robbed of worship; He was robbed of service; He was robbed of glory. But sadly enough, man was robbed too. Man was robbed of life, peace, and intimate fellowship with the Father. Thankfully, our God is in the restoration business.

Why did this *please* God? Did He want to see if Yeshua would present Himself as a guilt offering? Did He want to see if Yeshua was willing? Was it because back in Genesis He already knew we would fail, and He had already decided Yeshua would have to save us? He knew if He created us, we would fail, and Yeshua would have to come – for you and me. He would be *crushed* for us. How can we not appreciate that? *It pleased ADONAI to crush him with illness, to see if he would present himself as a guilt offering. If he does, he will see his offspring; and he will prolong his days; and at his hand ADONAI's desire will be accomplished* (Isaiah 53:10). This means you and I will be with Him forever, as He planned from the beginning. Not only were our sins atoned for, but our guilt is gone too.

This means you and I will be with Him forever, as He planned from the beginning.

In the gospel of John we read, *It was Preparation Day, and the Judeans did not want the bodies to remain on the stake on Shabbat* [Sabbath], *since it was an especially important Shabbat* (John 19:31). The Judeans here were the Jewish leaders. This didn't include all the Jews. Many of the Jewish people were different from the leadership because they loved Yeshua. The Jewish leaders didn't want the bodies hanging on the stakes over this Sabbath, a very special Sabbath, because it was during Passover. They asked Pilate to hasten their deaths by ordering their legs to be broken. This was in accordance with Deuteronomy 21:22-23, which says it's a curse to leave a man on a tree all night. *If someone has committed a capital crime and is put to death, then hung on a tree, his body is not to remain all night on the tree, but you must bury him the same day, because a person who has been hanged has been cursed by God.* They were just adhering to the Scriptures, but at the same time they were killing God's son. What a dichotomy! *So they asked Pilate to have the legs broken and the bodies removed. The soldiers came and broke the legs of*

*the first man who had been put on a stake beside Yeshua, then
the legs of the other one; but when they got to Yeshua and saw
that he was already dead, they didn't break his legs. However,
one of the soldiers stabbed his side with a spear, and at once
blood and water flowed out* (John 19:31-34).

The approaching Sabbath was a high Sabbath, because it
was during Passover: The request to remove the body was in
accordance with the Torah to not leave the body hanging on
the execution stake all night because it would defile the land.
The Romans typically crucified people, but the Jews could not.
The Romans were a gruesome people in the first century. Pilate
was so gruesome he killed family members or anybody who
disagreed with him. He was grotesque, evil, and abominable.

Many Jews sided with Yeshua, but the Jewish leadership
didn't like it. Yeshua was upsetting their apple cart and they
were threatened by Him. Their system of laws and traditions,
which they had created, was being disturbed, and their feath-
ers were being ruffled.

The Romans typically left the decaying bodies hanging on
the crosses long after their death – for days and days. However,
on certain occasions, like the emperor's birthday, they could
take the bodies down early if they facilitated a quick death
by breaking the legs. Philo, the historian, wrote about this in
Flaccus (X, 83).[13] By breaking the legs, the criminals couldn't
push themselves up to be able to breathe, so they would quickly
die of asphyxiation. The bones of crucified men were uncovered
in an excavation site near Jerusalem in 1968, and their legs were
in fact broken.[14] More and more historical and scientific proofs

13   Philo Judaeus, "Flaccus," *The Works of Philo. Early Christian Writings Online:*
      www.earlychristianwritings.com/ yonge/book36.html.
14   Biblical Archaeology Society Staff, "A Tomb in Jerusalem Reveals
      the History of Crucifixion and Roman Crucifixion Methods," *Bible
      History Daily: www.biblicalarchaeology.org/daily/biblical-topics/*

are being discovered that prove the Bible, so just because a person hasn't taken the time to see the evidence that demands a verdict, doesn't mean it's not true.

When the soldier pierced the side of Yeshua, blood and water came out, proving He was a normal human being. But notice that blood is mentioned first, then water. Remember how there are sixteen chapters in Exodus about the tabernacle, and everything in the tabernacle pointed to the heavenly tabernacle. The earthly tabernacle was symbolic of the heavenly tabernacle. More than that, we can take the Sermon on the Mount and almost superimpose it on the tabernacle and they become one. As soon as a person went in the first door, he had only entered the outer courtyard. Entering the door was voluntary; he didn't have to enter, but when he came in, he was saying, "I need You, God." This person was humbling himself before the Lord. Yeshua began His sermon in Matthew 5 with, *"How blessed are the poor in spirit! For the Kingdom of Heaven is theirs."* That's the first step – we must humble ourselves and come before God.

As soon as a Jewish person came into the outer courtyard, he saw the brazen altar. He had to bring an animal to the altar, which had a ramp in front of it. The brass of the altar was made of iron and copper, was very shiny, and gave a reflection. So as the man walked up the ramp and stood before the altar, he saw his own face. He recognized that he should be on the altar, not the innocent lamb. The copper in the altar speaks of being pliable, and the iron speaks of being strong. God's judgment is strong, but if we repent, it is pliable.

After the sacrifice was made on the brazen altar, the person

crucifixion/a-tomb-in-jerusalem-reveals-the-history-of-crucifixion-and-roman-crucifixion-methods/ (July 22, 2011).

66

moved to the laver and washed his hands. He was washing the guilt from his hands. We read in Leviticus that there were two goats for the day of Atonement. The priest laid his hands on the one and sliced it for the sin offering, and the other goat was the scapegoat that took the sin out of the camp (Leviticus 16:15-22).

However, the offering of all the goats, bulls, and rams couldn't cure us of our guilt. But surely, Yeshua's sacrifice, God's only Son, being completely shattered, could clear us of our guilt. *Now every cohen* [priest] *stands every day doing his service, offering over and over the same sacrifices, which can never take away sins. But this one, after he had offered for all time a single sacrifice for sins, sat down at the right hand of God, from then on to wait until his enemies be made a footstool for his feet* (Hebrews 10:11-13). The Scripture states *the priest stands doing his service,* because he's never finished. Yeshua, on the other hand, *sat down at God's right hand.* Halleluyah. Our guilt is gone, because IT IS FINISHED! That's one of the hardest things to accept. Yeshua took away our guilt – just like that. Wrapping our minds around this might not be totally possible, but it's true. When we think about Yeshua laying down His life and getting completely shattered to bridge the chasm between God and us, this is a life-changing revelation. It's over the top and too much to comprehend.

> **Wrapping our minds around this might not be totally possible, but it's true.**

Chapter 4

A Sacrifice, Living and Set Apart for God

The Number Five

We've seen how the five offerings in Leviticus point to Yeshua, and in fact, all roads in the Bible point to Yeshua. *Five* is important because it always speaks of grace, and as we've looked at the five offerings, we've not only seen the price He paid, but we've also seen that through His grace we are able to live a life for God now.

Having discussed the five offerings, I find it interesting to also note that there are five kinds of wounds known to medical science: contusions, lacerations, penetrating wounds, perforating wounds, and incised wounds. Not only did all five offerings point to Yeshua, but Yeshua suffered all five types of wounds.

Isaiah 53 will always be a significant chapter, because it speaks of the suffering servant in great detail and says He was wounded. *But he was wounded because of our crimes* (Isaiah

53:5). There's the word *wounded*. If he was wounded because of our crimes, we need to understand these wounds.

Contusions

The first wound is a contusion. This is an injury caused by a blunt instrument which damages the tissue below the surface of the skin. We call these injuries "bruises." The blood capillaries, which are the smallest blood vessels in our bodies, rupture when they're struck, but the skin is not broken. Matthew 27:30 says, *They spit on him and used the stick to beat him about the head.* Simply put, they beat Yeshua with a stick, which caused bruising.

Lacerations

A laceration is totally different. It's a deep cut or a tear in the skin that causes the tissue to be mangled. *Pilate then took Yeshua and had him flogged* (John 19:1). Look at how short that sentence is with so little information about this flogging. Pilate was such a horrible person that there were many uprisings, so we can assume this flogging wasn't an easy whipping. We don't really get a picture of what took place during these floggings unless we dig deeper into history to learn about the actual practice. The word *scourging* is sometimes used in place of *flogging* and portrays what a horrific, cruel punishment it was.

The people who carried out the floggings were professionals, trained young men called *lictors*, because they were experts at inflicting pain. They tied their victims in an X position and used a flagellum to beat them. *Flagellum* is a Latin word for a long whip with curved, broken pieces of bone or pottery connected to the tail. So the skilled professional lictor hit the victim, and the whip grabbed the flesh and left long lacerations. It tore and mangled the skin so deep that it even grabbed the insides of the person to expose bones and intestines as the lictor pulled back. Flogging, or scourging, was known as halfway-death, because the person was left almost dead, but not quite. The lictors were so professional they knew when to stop just short of death.[15]

The Greek word for flog is *masti-goo*, and it means "to scourge." The root word in the Greek is *mastix* and

> I think sometimes the cross loses its power, because we talk about it so matter-of-factly.

means "a calamity or a disaster," but it refers to God sending severe pain in the best eternal interests of the victim. It was discipline from God to help us understand here that Yeshua was being disciplined by His Father – He was being punished.

Going back to Isaiah, we see that it says, *In fact, it was our diseases he bore, our pains from which he suffered . . . the disciplining that makes us whole fell on him, and by his bruises we are healed* (Isaiah 53:4-5). He suffered for our pains; His disciplining and flogging are what makes us whole.

As a side note, I spoke to a pastor recently and shared much of this with him. He was like most pastors in his denomination and preached the cross regularly. He asked how a Jew from New York could understand the depths of the cross; I told him because this Jew from New York spends a lot of time at the cross. I think sometimes the cross loses its power, because we talk about it so matter-of-factly. I think God loses His power, because we talk about Him matter-of-factly. We don't approach Him with reverence, and we don't open our Bibles. Like the

---

15 William D. Edwards, MD, et al., "Scourging and Crucifixion In Roman Tradition," *Truth of God: www.cbcg.org/ scourging-crucifixion.html.*

song that says, "I'll never know how much it cost," sometimes I
think we've lost our passion, our great remorse, for what it cost.

Penetrating Wounds

The next set of wounds are the penetrating wounds, open
wounds caused by a deep piercing of the skin. Once again, we
can see clearly how Yeshua experienced this.

> *They stripped off his clothes and put on him a scarlet*
> *robe, wove thorn-branches into a crown and put it on*
> *his head, and put a stick in his right hand. Then they*
> *kneeled down in front of him and made fun of him:*
> *"Hail to the King of the Jews!"* (Matthew 27:28-29)

So they stripped off His clothes and put a scarlet robe on Him,
which was a *chlamys*, a very short robe that barely covered the
genitalia and was used as a mockery. Then they wove a crown
from branches with thorns at least three inches long, very
strong, and couldn't be broken. When
they put it on His head, they pressed
it into His head, causing penetrating
wounds. They placed a stick in His
hand as a pretend scepter and knelt
down before Him to mock Him, which
was part of all of the shame, but we
know that *God raised him to the high-*
est place and gave him the name above
every name; that in honor of the name given Yeshua, every knee
will bow – in heaven, on earth and under the earth – and every
tongue will acknowledge that Yeshua the Messiah is ADONAI *to*
the glory of God the Father (Philippians 2:9-11). Even though

**Even though these
soldiers mocked Yeshua
and beat Him while He
was on the earth, one
day all knees will honor
Him by bowing to Him.**

these soldiers mocked Yeshua and beat Him while He was on the earth, one day all knees will honor Him by bowing to Him.

Perforating Wounds

The fourth set of wounds are the perforating wounds, which are injuries made by making holes through boring. They puncture the skin, enter the body cavity or appendage, and exit the body on the other side. A perforating trauma can be caused by a foreign object or by fragments of a broken bone. They usually occur in violent crime or armed combat. John 19:17-18 says, *Carrying the stake himself he went out to the place called Skull (in Aramaic, Gulgolta). There they nailed him to the stake along with two others, one on either side, with Yeshua in the middle.* He carried the stake Himself. Imagine how incredibly exhausted one would be, half dead from the flogging but still having to carry this heavy stake. He went out to a place called Skull, and they nailed Him to the stake along with two others.

Roman Crucifixion

Crucifixion was widely practiced by the Romans. The Jews weren't allowed to crucify anybody, but the Roman authority developed and used it on many criminals. The early historian Josephus, who is as highly regarded as any historian in the history of historians, mentions thousands of people being crucified in first-century Israel, mostly during the rebellions against Rome. And calling yourself a king was the ultimate rebellion, which the governors wouldn't tolerate because Caesar was their king.

Stories indicate that Roman soldiers played cruel games with different postures for their crucified victims. The use of nails in a crossbar was the most common, but sometimes they just impaled the victims. Being suspended by one's arms, whether nailed or impaled, caused great difficulty in breathing. The modern medical explanation for the cause of death on the cross is asphyxiation or shock, but usually a combination of both. The victims pushed themselves up, using a small block of wood below their feet, to be able to inhale some air and take the weight off their arms, but that small motion itself caused incredible pain – in the arms, the legs, the feet, and the back. After they gasped the air in, the legs of the exhausted victims gave out, and they slumped over once more, unable to breathe with all their weight back on their wrists. This same horrific movement happened over and over. Up and down, gasping for air, and causing excruciating pain.[16] We can't even imagine it. Eventually, the victims succumbed to suffocation.

Crucifixion was widely believed to be the worst form of execution due to the excruciating pain and public shame. Marcus Tullius Cicero, (106-43 BC), the greatest orator of the Roman Republic and a brilliant lawyer, wrote about crucifixion. When crucifixion is compared to other forms of execution, such as being boiled in oil or being burned at the stake, he found that crucifixion was the worst form of execution, because it caused the most intense pain for the longest duration.

Incised Wounds

An incised wound is a deep wound caused by sharp-force trauma with a knife or spear. We've already seen that Yeshua was already dead when the soldiers came to break His legs, but they couldn't resist thrusting a spear into His side. *It was Preparation Day . . . but when they got to Yeshua and saw that he was already dead, they didn't break his legs. However, one of*

---

16   *www.tribunesandtriumphs.org/roman-life/roman-crucifixion.htm.*

the soldiers stabbed his side with a spear, and at once blood and water flowed out (John 19:31, 33-34).

Did you ever wonder why the soldiers didn't break Yeshua's legs even though He was dead? Why did they thrust that spear into his side? Did the Israelites understand what it meant when Yeshua's legs weren't broken? John tells us that these things happened, so Scripture would be fulfilled. Consider the words of Psalm 34:20: *He protects all his bones; not one of them gets broken,* and also Exodus 12:46 where it speaks of the Passover Lamb: *It is to be eaten in one house. You are not to take any of the meat outside the house, and you are not to break any of its bones.* Because Yeshua was their Passover Lamb, none of His bones could be broken. That's why John exclaimed, *Look! God's lamb! The one who is taking away the sin of the world!* (John 1:29).

> These wounds cover the whole spectrum of possible wounds that Yeshua could experience, and His sacrifice covers the whole spectrum of possible sins of the human race.

Zechariah 12:10 tells us, *they will look to me, whom they pierced.* By thrusting his spear into the side of Yeshua, the soldier actually fulfilled the prophecy of Zechariah. And from this wound, blood and water flowed, blood for the forgiveness of sin and water for the washing away of the guilt of our sin. If we recall the brazen altar and laver, we realize that Yeshua fulfilled that requirement for approaching the Father. The blood was shed at the altar, and the guilt washed away at the laver, just as the blood and water flowed from Yeshua's side. He laid down His own life as a voluntary act. The incised wound was one of the last prophecies to be fulfilled while Yeshua was on earth.

These wounds cover the whole spectrum of possible wounds

that Yeshua could experience, and His sacrifice covers the whole spectrum of possible sins of the human race. He needed to be wounded in all these ways to heal the whole world of all of its sin. The word *heal* is from the Hebrew word *rapha* meaning "to heal," but the figurative use of this word in the Hebrew means "restored favor," which involved spiritual healing.

Is physical healing necessary or possible? Yeshua asked what good it would be to go to hell with two good eyes, two good arms, and two good legs. He said, *"And if your eye makes you sin, pluck it out! Better that you should be one-eyed but enter the Kingdom of God, rather than keep both eyes and be thrown into Gei-Hinnom* [hell]" (Mark 9:47). Physical healing isn't the most important thing, but we do see it. On occasion, blind people have instantaneously opened their eyes and seen, or people in their seventies and eighties, bent over with age and arthritis, have straightened up and walked. But these occasions often happen in countries where the people need to see the power of God before they receive Him. Above all, God wants to heal the heart.

Above all, God wants to heal the heart.

When I travel to remote places and can show in a physical way that my God is more powerful than their god, they will listen to me. Healing was the carrot God used to get them in a position to hear and believe. We are already healed and don't need physical healing in order to hear. We've already been restored to favor with the Father by the bruises of Yeshua if we've humbled ourselves before Him and accepted the sacrifice He made on our behalf.

The length of our lives really doesn't matter. No matter how many surgeries we might have or age-defying methods we use, one out of one of us will still die. But although we die, we live, and we have something to look forward to after this life. We have a blessed hope, and that's the anchor, the ultimate anchor, to our soul. Our humble desire is to give all of ourselves to Yeshua, to sit at His table for the meal offering, and fellowship with Him. The apostle Paul in his letter to the Romans said, *I exhort you, therefore, brothers, in view of God's mercies, to offer yourselves as a sacrifice, living and set apart for God* (Romans 12:1).

We want to have a relationship with God, a conversation, all the days of our lives, but there's a chasm that needs to be bridged. The fact of the matter is that we can't make restitution for all of our sins. We can't bridge that chasm. *What a miserable creature I am! Who will rescue me from this body bound for death? Thanks be to God, [he will]! – through Yeshua the Messiah, our Lord!* (Romans 7:24-25). So we either have to accept Yeshua's sacrifice for our sins, or we are responsible for it.

Yeshua's Mission

As a side note, we should recognize that Yeshua knew what His mission was – it was no surprise. Yeshua *asked his talmidim* [disciples] . . . *"who do you say I am?" Shim'on Kefa* [Simon Peter] *answered, "You are the Mashiach* [Messiah], *the Son of the living God"* (Matthew 16:13, 15-16). Peter realized that Yeshua wasn't just a great Rabbi or a great teacher. He wasn't just a great guy. He was the Messiah. This was the first time Yeshua was recognized, and He told Peter that flesh and blood hadn't revealed that to him, but His Father had. *How blessed you are! For no human being revealed this to you, no, it was my Father in heaven* (Matthew 16:17). From that time on, Yeshua made it very clear what His goal was. He didn't speak in parables and riddles to them. He told them He had to go to Jerusalem, endure much suffering at the hands of the elders, and be put to death. But He gave them hope – He would be raised again on the third day.

> *We are now going up to Yerushalayim* [Jerusalem],
> *where the Son of Man will be handed over to the head*
> *cohanim* [chief priests] *and Torah-teachers* [scribes].
> *They will sentence him to death and turn him over to*
> *the Goyim* [Gentiles]. (Matthew 20:18-19)

These Jewish leaders couldn't kill Him, so they turned Him over to the Gentiles who beat Him, mocked Him, and killed Him on a stake. But once again, He gave them hope. He said, *"But on the third day, he will be raised"* (Matthew 20:19).

Yeshua clarified His purpose even more when he said, *"For the Son of Man did not come to be served, but to serve – and to give his life as a ransom for many"* (Matthew 20:28). He didn't come to be served; He came to serve. To be the ultimate servant, He gave His life as a ransom. We were ransomed because Yeshua knew His mission and kept His eyes on the goal – the salvation of miserable human beings. Luke 19:10 says, *For the Son of Man came to seek and save what was lost.* That was why He came – not to put on a show or heal people. He was on a rescue mission.

Another part of Yeshua's mission was to make it possible for us to know His Father. "Jesus-Only" Christians seem to have missed the mark. When the disciples wanted to learn to pray, Yeshua told them to address His Father – their Father – our Father. He said, *"Pray like this: 'Our Father in heaven!'"* (Matthew 6:9). Yeshua is our connection to the Father; He is the Star of David; He is our Mediator. *For God is one; and there is but one Mediator between God and humanity, Yeshua the Messiah* (1 Timothy 2:5). Yeshua came in flesh and blood to connect us with the Father; everybody needs a Father. In the book of Hebrews, we learn that *we have a great cohen gadol* [high priest] *who has passed through to the highest heaven, Yeshua, so we can confidently approach the throne from which God gives grace, so that we may receive mercy and find grace in our time of need* (Hebrews 4:14, 16).

Don't be fooled into thinking that because Yeshua was totally divine, His suffering on the cross was an easy task for Him. Although He was fully divine as the Son of God, He was also fully man. So when Yeshua was hungry, thirsty, or tired, it was real pain just like we experience. The crucifixion was horrific, and the pain and suffering were absolutely brutal. We've seen how horrible the crucifixion was physically, but

> Don't be fooled into thinking that because Yeshua was totally divine, His suffering on the cross was an easy task for Him.

what about the emotional and mental anguish? Luke tells us that *in great anguish he prayed more intensely, so that his sweat became like drops of blood falling to the ground* (Luke 22:44). Look at that word *anguish*, which comes from the Greek word *agónia*, and we get our English word *agony* from it. It means "severe mental and emotional struggle and stress." Luke called this *great* anguish – as if normal anguish isn't bad enough. How great? He prayed so intensely that his sweat became like drops of blood, and it fell to the ground.

The medical term for this is *hematidrosis* or *hematohidrosis*, and it occurs when the blood vessels, which form a net-like structure around the sweat glands, constrict when under the pressure of great stress. When the anxiety passes, the vessels dilate to the point of rupturing, and the blood flows into the sweat glands. As the glands produce more sweat, they push the blood to the surface, forming droplets of blood mixed with sweat. This is a rare but very real phenomenon.

After all of this suffering and pain, *At about three, Yeshua uttered a loud cry, "Eli! Eli! L'mah sh'vaktani? (My God! My God! Why have you deserted me?)"* (Matthew 27:46). Yeshua cried this out with a loud cry – He didn't whisper. Why did He cry so loud when He was in such a weakened state? He must have wanted everybody to hear it and record it. Why was it that important? The word *deserted* means "to abandon and leave helpless." Note the beginning of Psalm 22: *My God! My God! Why have you abandoned me? Why so far from helping me, so far from my anguished cries?* He's not asking God why He's allowing Him to be nailed to the cross, though that was extremely painful. The mental and emotional stress of knowing He was going to take on the sins of the world and for the first time in His life be separated from His Father was what caused Him to cry out.

We've never had unbroken fellowship with the Father. We break it all the time, but we know *If we acknowledge our sins, then, since he is trustworthy and just, he will forgive them and purify us from all wrongdoing* (1 John 1:9). Not only that, but John tells us, *My children, I am writing you these things so that you won't sin. But if anyone does sin, we have Yeshua the Messiah, the Tzaddik* [Righteous], *who pleads our cause with the Father* (1 John 2:1). It's imperative that we see John address us as *my children*. It tells us that we always have relationship, but we don't always have fellowship.

Look at the word *abandon* in Psalm 22. In the Hebrew, it means "to depart from, to leave, to neglect." This is a very dark, horrifying reality because Yeshua had always been One with His Father. At this point, there is separation; He's been totally cut off. Why? First, God is holy, and when it comes to sin, He can't overlook it, wink at it, or brush it under the rug. God's holiness is pillar number one. Second, God is love, and Yeshua totally volunteered to pay the penalty. The two pillars are God is holy and God is love.

Remember what words were written on the two pillars of Solomon's temple? One was *Jachin*, meaning "God establishes." The other was *Boaz*, meaning "strength." He was telling us that we will get into the Holy of Holies because He's going to establish it in His strength. It's going to be a total gift and a total act of grace. God is going to establish His kingdom, and we're going to get into that kingdom by the grace of His strength.

> We often think about the anguish of the Son, but what about the Father?

Now imagine the mental, emotional, and spiritual anguish of the Father as He watched His Son suffer and die. Imagine the pillars of the temple being God's legs, and God Himself would be behind the veil in the Holy of Holies. God tore that veil from top to bottom like it was His shirt, as a sign of His grief and mourning. We often think about the anguish of the Son, but what about the Father? Imagine His agony.

What if our house was burning, and we came running to save our child, but the firemen said it was too late. We couldn't go in, but we could hear the horrific cries of our child. What grief! What agony! What about the Father? The whole thing was painful for Him and for Yeshua. The star maker became the sin taker.

Think about all of these wounds and all of this suffering, very real suffering. If the price was this vast, how much you are loved! And how valuable you are to God! Shouldn't we give serious consideration to the bidding of Yeshua in Matthew 16:25? *For whoever wants to save his own life will destroy it, but whoever destroys his life for my sake will find it.* May we choose to live for eternity – may we live for God.

Chapter 5

The Height and Depth of the Messiah's Love

The Number Three

As the number *five* pictured God's grace in the sacrifices and wounds, the number *three* speaks of divine perfection. In the Bible, we see the tripartite: the Father, the Son, and the Holy Spirit (Matthew 28:19). God's number is *three*. This number appears hundreds of times in Scripture. For example, all men are descended from Shem, Ham, and Japheth, the three sons of Noah (Genesis 9:18-19). Abraham, Isaac, and Jacob (Israel) were the three patriarchs of the nation of Israel. The tabernacle was divided into the outer court, the Holy Place, and the Holy of Holies. The three items held in the ark of the covenant were the pot of manna, Aaron's rod, and the Ten Commandments (Hebrews 9:4). Time exists as past, present, and future. Jonah was in the belly of the fish for three days and three nights, and the Son of Man was three days and three nights in the depths of the earth (Matthew 12:40).

Yeshua's earthly ministry began as He was tempted by Satan in three different ways (Matthew 4:1-11). Yeshua declared, *I AM the Way – and the Truth and the Life* (John 14:6). He was crucified at the third hour (Mark 15:25). Then He was resurrected on the third day (Luke 24:6-7).

Psalm 22, Psalm 23, and Psalm 24 also form a tripartite. Psalm 22 begins, *My God! My God! Why have you abandoned me?* That's the crucifixion and points to the Good Shepherd; it's in the past. Psalm 23 begins, *ADONAI* [The Lord] *is my shepherd*; this is the God who is, the Holy Spirit dwelling in us. He makes us lie down even in the midst of horrific situations. He is the Great Shepherd. Then in Psalm 24, we have the God who will be, the One who is returning to us. He is the Chief Shepherd. In these three Psalms, we see the Passover, Shavuot (Pentecost), and Sukkot (Feast of Tabernacles). Right there in the Psalms we have the God who was, the God who is, and the God who is to come. But you can't have the God who is to come unless you have the God who was.

> You can't have the God who is to come unless you have the God who was.

The Mournful Lament

Some people read Psalm 22 as a lament, just a mournful lament in its Old Testament context where the suffering of this individual is totally unwarranted and intensified by the jeering and mockery towards the sufferer. Others see this psalm as prophetically speaking about the crucifixion. One can see the psalmist providing a lament for the innocent sufferer and then see how the gospel writers used the lament to picture the ultimate sufferer, the prophesied Messiah who would suffer and die for the sins of the world and restore mankind to God. Psalm 22 was penned over a thousand years before the crucifixion and about five hundred years before crucifixion was even used by the rulers of the land, but we can easily see its prophetic nature and implications.[17]

Charles Spurgeon wrote of this prophetic aspect of the psalm in *The Treasury of David*. Spurgeon was born in 1834 but only lived fifty-seven years. He was called the Prince of Preachers even though he went through many bouts of depression. Many men of God have battled depression. Jeremiah certainly experienced depression as did Jonathan Edwards. Any man who stands on the Word of God in an uncompromising, unswerving manner and does all he can to glorify and please God without being concerned with what men say will likely go through bouts of depression.

Often tens of thousands of people came out to hear Charles Spurgeon, and his sermons were printed in the *London Times*. He was so unswerving that he broke with the Church of England and also left the Baptists. He was *sola Scriptura*, meaning Scripture alone is the primary and absolute source for doctrine and practice. He believed that if it wasn't in the Word of God, it wasn't worth talking about.

Two points Spurgeon preached over and over. The first was the restoration of Israel because he knew that God was going to restore the land to the Jewish people. He didn't know when, but he knew it would happen. He knew the people would come back to the Promised Land, which they did. And in 1948, Israel became an independent state.

---

17   *www.bible.ca/d-history-archeology-crucifixion-cross.htm.*

Secondly, Spurgeon was also confident that Messiah would return to Jerusalem and usher in the times of refreshing:

But this is how God fulfilled what he had announced in advance, when he spoke through all the prophets, namely, that his Messiah was to die. "Therefore, repent and turn to God, so that your sins may be erased; so that times of refreshing may come from the Lord's presence; and he may send the Messiah appointed in advance for you, that is, Yeshua. He has to remain in heaven until the time comes for restoring everything, as God said long ago, when he spoke through the holy prophets. (Acts 3:18-21)

In his commentary on the Psalms, Spurgeon said, "For plaintive [mournful] expressions uprising from unutterable depths of woe we may say of this psalm, 'there is none like it.' It is the photograph of our Lord's saddest hours, the record of his dying words, the lachrymatory of his last tears, the memorial of his expiring joys."[18] A lachrymatory, or lachrymal, was a small vase used in Roman tombs in the first century to collect the tears of those who came to mourn at funerals. They did this to let the person know and let God know they didn't die in vain. Spurgeon went on to say, "We should read reverently [with great holiness], putting off our shoes from off our feet, as Moses did at the burning bush, for if there be holy ground anywhere in Scripture it is in this psalm."[19]

Let's look at verses 1 and 2. *My God! My God! Why have you abandoned me? Why so far from helping me, so far from*

---

18   Charles Spurgeon, "Psalm 22," *The Treasury of David: www.spurgeon.org/treasury/treasury.php.*
19   Ibid.

my anguished cries? My God, by day I call to you, but you don't answer; likewise at night, but I get no relief.

Take note of how much the punctuation adds to this. He wasn't whispering to God. He called out in a loud voice. Then we see a question – He wanted to know *why* He'd been abandoned. The commas tell us to pause and think before hurrying on. He'd called to God day and night but didn't receive an answer.

> He wasn't whispering to God. He called out in a loud voice.

This is real life; this happens to us. We go through times when we cry out to God day and night, and we don't hear Him. We get no relief.

Notice also the question that He opened with. *Why?* That's always a tough question, and He wanted to know why God wouldn't help Him. He wondered why God didn't answer. Why no relief? How often do we ask God, "Why?" We don't understand, and we want to hear from Him.

Agony of the Father

Psalm 22 tells us about the longest, darkest, most horrible three hours of Yeshua's earthly existence and the darkest, most horrible hours of the earth itself. Now, as right as it is to focus on Yeshua here, we can't forget the Father. The Father watched this from heaven. He looked down and saw His only begotten Son, very much a part of Him, being used as a scapegoat for man's sins. Not only that, but they didn't even appreciate it. The Father gave His Son while they jeered and mocked and said His punishment and death were because of His sin. What was the Father to do? What would you do if they were torturing your child, and you were right there? Then they mocked and laughed and goofed around. What would you do? Would you fight back?

What did the Father do? He deliberately unleashed all His fury and all His righteous wrath on Him, the Son. Why did He do that? The next verse gives us the answer: *Nevertheless, you are holy, enthroned on the praises of Isra'el* (Psalm 22:3).

He unleashed His fury because He is holy. That's why we couldn't do the same because we're not holy. We could never give that much or love like that because we're finite beings. But Yeshua reminded God here that the ancestors cried out, and He answered them, and they weren't always holy. *In you our ancestors put their trust; they trusted, and you rescued them. They cried to you and escaped; they trusted in you and were not disappointed.* (Psalm 22:5-6).

God isn't just a covenant maker; He's a covenant keeper, and He has to keep His covenant. In Genesis 1:26, God said, *Let us make humankind in our image, in the likeness of ourselves.* Only God has the power to create. So what does the word *us* mean? Man wasn't created yet, so it couldn't mean him. Clearly, He wasn't speaking to the animal kingdom or the plant kingdom. Knowing the Hebrew here helps us understand what He was saying. Literally, it is "shall we?" The Hebrew word for God here is *Elohim*, the plural form of *Eloah*. So in the Hebrew, He's almost talking to Himself because there's a plurality about God. This is a plural unity or a unified plurality.

In other words God can be in the heavens, on the heavens, and everywhere else, and still be in His fullness and manifest His presence anywhere He wants. So, He was discussing with Himself if He wanted to create man. He knew we were going to sin, and since He is holy and He is love, He knew He would want to save us. He knew He would have to take a piece of

Himself, send it in human form, unleash His fury on Him, and crush Him. The next verse gives God's answer: *So God created humankind in his own image; in the image of God he created him: male and female he created them* (Genesis 1:27). He made me and you, knowing we would need a Savior.

Then we get the first Messianic prophecy in Genesis 3:15. *I will put animosity between you and the woman, and between your descendant and her descendant; he will bruise your head, and you will bruise his heel.* God said He would put hostility between Satan and the woman and between his offspring and her offspring, which is Yeshua. It will be the anti-Messiah against the Messiah. There will be

> It's either the kingdom of light or the kingdom of darkness. There's no third choice.

hatred and animosity. If you're in the word, it's either black or white. It's either the kingdom of light or the kingdom of darkness. There's no third choice. He's saying that they're going to hate us, and we're going to hate them. Yes, it's right to hate evil. That is something we can hate, but God said the woman's offspring would bruise the head of Satan. That's a death blow.

Then in Genesis 12, God said He would bless all the families of the earth. All the way back in early Genesis, God planned to work it out so He would show up on earth in human form and die for the sins of the world, and every family would be blessed. Think about how He had to orchestrate history to make everything come together at the right time and in the right place. Think about how many times Satan tried to exterminate all the Jews when they were banished and exiled. They disappear; they come back; they disappear; they come back. God will keep His promise to them to give them their land forever.

The Crimson Worm

We see how from the very beginning God had a plan, and it involved Yeshua being forsaken by the Father. That's what we see in the beginning of Psalm 22. Then verse 6 says, *But I am a worm, not a man, scorned by everyone, despised by the people.* A worm? In the middle of speaking of being tortured and abandoned, He said He's a worm, a lowly creature. This means more than just feeling like a nobody. A worm is a helpless, powerless, downtrodden creature. It's the lowest of all creatures – all flesh and no bone. When downtrodden, the worm writhes and twists its body in extreme pain. That's all worms do; they quiver and twist until they are utterly devoid of any might. Powerless, except for the strength to suffer.

A worm is also a biblical symbol for depravity, meaning morally wrong. That doesn't seem to make sense when referring to Yeshua, but the Hebrew word for this worm is *tola.* There are two definitions for this word, and this particular worm is called the crimson worm. Scientifically it's called the *coccus illicis.* This Hebrew word also refers to the dye made from the dried body of the coccus illicis. Did you ever wonder how they got the red or purple dye they used in the temple? They used the dye from the coccus illicis.

When the worm is ready to give birth, she voluntarily attaches her body to the trunk of a very specific tree. She fixes herself so firmly and permanently, she can never leave again. In Psalm 22:6, Yeshua referred to himself as the crimson worm, the coccus illicis, but few people understand the significance of this. The eggs that are deposited beneath her body are protected until the larvae hatch and are able to reach their own cycle of life. As the mother dies, the crimson fluid stains her body, the eggs, and the wood.

There are three points that are quite compelling in this illustration. First, the crimson worm climbs onto a very specific tree all by itself. Nobody forces her to get on this tree. The worm does this by its own free will.

For years, many people have said that Jesus died for their sins, but we often overlook something significant. Jesus died because He was totally faithful to the Father, totally obedient. His motivation was to please the Father; that's why He died. *This is why the Father loves me: because I lay down my life – in order to take it up again! No one takes it away from me; on the contrary, I lay it down of my own free will* (John 10:17-18).

> Jesus died because He was totally faithful to the Father, totally obedient. His motivation was to please the Father; that's why He died.

If we were more like Him, instead of doing for others, our desire would be to obey the Father. In turn, we'd be doing for others, but ultimately our goal would be to please the Father. We don't have to have a checklist of things to do, because our checklist is to bring pleasure to the Father, and He will lead us to do what He wants us to do.

The specific tree that the worm searches for is the Kermes Oak tree, which is only found in the Mediterranean. This tree is the worm's destiny; it knows which tree it's going to – to give her life. When the disciples finally figured out that Yeshua was Messiah, He explained to them what was to come: *From that time on, Yeshua began making it clear to his talmidim [disciples] that he had to go to Yerushalayim [Jerusalem] and endure much suffering at the hands of the elders, the head cohanim [chief priests] and the Torah-teachers* (Matthew 16:21). He had to do this; He had no choice, just like there's no choice in that crimson worm, the coccus illicis. She has to go to that tree to die, which is her destiny. The cross was His destiny.

The chief priests, the leaders of the Jews but not the Jewish people, gave Him up to be tortured and killed. Why did it have to be the chief priests and leaders? They were the ones who instituted and performed the sacrificial system, so they had to present the sacrifice. It's biblical, it's Levitical, and it's right. Nobody else could put their hands on Him because they were presenting the offering for Israel and the world.

After the crimson worm dies, it can be scraped from the tree, and the crimson gel can be used to make red and purple dye. This is the same dye used in the tabernacle and for the priestly garments. In Exodus 25:1-2, it says, *ADONAI said to Moshe* [Moses], *Tell the people of Isra'el to take up a collection for me – accept a contribution from anyone who wholeheartedly wants to give.* Chapters 25 through 40 all cover the tabernacle – the construction, the furniture, the priests and their garments, and their offerings. Sixteen chapters! God is telling us that this is important. He wanted it built exactly as He told them, because it was to be a copy of the tabernacle in heaven.

Notice that God didn't want anything that was given begrudgingly. He wanted the people to give wholeheartedly.

Next, notice that God didn't want anything that was given begrudgingly. He wanted the people to give wholeheartedly. He said, *The contribution you are to take from them is to consist of gold, silver and bronze; blue, purple and scarlet yarn* (Exodus 25:3-4). The precious metals of gold, silver, and bronze were needed for the laver, the silver trumpets, and the gold that covered the ark of the covenant. Then we have blue, purple, scarlet, which had to be dyed, and white – the four colors of the veil that separated the Holy Place from the Holy of Holies, God's presence.

The Number Four

The number *four* also has significance. We have four colors, four creatures, and four gospels, and they all connect. The gospel of Matthew begins with the Jewish genealogy, because He wrote to the Jewish people to show them Yeshua was a Jew, a son of Abraham, a son of Isaac, a son of David. Matthew wanted to show them He was the prophesied Jewish Messiah, the King of Israel, the King of the Jews. He talks about Yeshua's royalty, and purple is the color for royalty.

The gospel of Luke was written to the Greeks who were looking for perfection in man. They were great philosophers and strove to figure out how they could be perfect. White depicts perfection and purity.

Blue is representative of John's gospel, because it's the universal gospel. Blue speaks of the heavens, and John depicts Yeshua not as the Son of Man, but as the Son of God from the heavens.

Red represents Mark's gospel, because Mark is short on doctrine but huge on miracles. It's powerful. The Romans wanted a suffering servant, and they wanted a bull, because they were proud of their strength, the people who gave their lives for Rome, and the great empire. The red signified the giving of those lives.

Then we have the four living creatures. The lion signified royalty and is represented by the color purple. White represents man and purity. The eagle is represented by the blue of the heavens, the Son of God. And the bull represented the sacrifice, the red. Every time we see red in the tabernacle, it's representative of sacrifice, of suffering, of atonement, and of blood. The blood is for cleansing as we know there is no remission of sin without blood. *In fact, according to the Torah, almost everything is puri-fied with blood; indeed, without the shedding of blood there is no forgiveness of sins* (Hebrews 9:22).

Separation from the Father

But you are the one who took me from the womb, you made me trust when I was on my mother's breasts. Since my birth I've been thrown on you; you are my God from my mother's womb. Don't stay far from me, for trouble is near; and there is no one to help. (Psalm 22:9-11)

Remember when Yeshua was born and the magi, the men from the East, came? They were just astronomers and astrologers. Where do you think they got their information from? Do you suppose Daniel spoke to them when he was there? Maybe they passed on to their sons, who passed on to their sons, what Daniel had told them – that a very special star, a messianic star, would appear. Maybe Daniel told them to keep watching for that star and to follow it when it appeared. And those men from the East came, but they were warned in a dream not to go back to Herod because Herod wanted to kill Yeshua. *But they had been warned in a dream not to return to Herod, so they took another route back to their own country* (Matthew 2:12). If Herod could destroy Yeshua, there would be no Messiah. So what Yeshua was saying in Psalm 22 was that the Father was there even at birth. He was always there. Yeshua was never disconnected from the Father

He was never attracted to anything that distracted Him from the mission He was on.

because He was never attracted to anything that distracted Him from the mission He was on.

In verse 11, however, He cried out for the Father's presence. Trouble was near and there was no one to help. Yeshua declared that He needed the Father more than ever, but He didn't know where the Father was. Because Yeshua was totally man, He had given up certain things – He was totally dependent on the Father and the Spirit. In His humanness, He was in pain and experienced sadness and sorrow. Even though He had the Spirit without measure, He was human and felt abandoned, so He cried for His Father to return to Him. *I am poured out like water; all my bones are out of joint; my heart has become like wax – it melts inside me; my mouth is as dry as a fragment of a pot, my tongue sticks to my palate; you lay me down in the dust of death* (Psalm 22:14-15).

Yeshua was saying He was totally done in, completely exhausted. When He said, *all my bones are out of joint,* He was referring to the crucifixion, because when a body hangs like that, the shoulders, hips, and knees dislocate. The pull on those joints for hours and hours was awful. We know His internal organs were malfunctioning, because He said His heart had become like wax, melting within Him. His mouth was parched, and His tongue stuck to His palate. By this point, Yeshua had no strength – His body had shut down, and His bones were completely out of joint. Then in verses 16 to 18, He said, *Dogs are all around me, a pack of villains closes in on me like a lion [at] my hands and feet. I can count every one of my bones, while they gaze at me and gloat. They divide my garments among themselves; for my clothing they throw dice.*

These verses speak of the extreme humiliation of being on display in front of these *dogs,* these non-Jews. But look at verse

18. *They divide my garments.* Mark 15:24 tells us, *Then they nailed him to the execution-stake; and they divided his clothes among themselves, throwing dice to determine what each man should get.* But Yeshua made one last cry to the Father for help in Psalm 22:19-20. *But you, ADONAI, don't stay far away! My strength, come quickly to help me! Rescue me from the sword, my life from the power of the dogs.*

In Yeshua's last plea, He asked for His strength to come quickly, and His strength was His God. *ADONAI is my strength and shield* (Psalm 28:7). He was nothing without the Father, but He is everything with Him.

> Take the time and do it, and consider living your life for God – for eternity.

For a moment consider the crucifixion of this innocent man, the Son of God; consider the flagellum and the flogging, the humiliation, and the agony of separation. It will change your heart, and it will change your walk. Take the time and do it, and consider living your life for God – for eternity.

The New Covenant

God told Jeremiah He would make a new covenant with the Jewish people. Once again, God would do it. He said:

> *"Here, the days are coming," says ADONAI, "when I will make a new covenant with the house of Isra'el and with the house of Y'hudah [Judah]. It will not be like the covenant I made with their fathers on the day I took them by their hand and brought them out of the land of Egypt; because they, for their part, violated my covenant, even though I, for*

my part, was a husband to them," says ADONAI.
(Jeremiah 31:31-32)

We see here that Israel and Judah are not going to be replaced, because God is obviously not done with them. Romans 11 indicates that when the fullness of the Gentiles has come, God will resume His plan to fulfill His covenant with Israel.

God had made that covenant with their forefathers when He gave them His law and promised to bless them. But what did they say? They said, "Tell Moses, and we will obey." Did they? No. But in His grace and mercy, God decided to establish a new covenant. He promised to put it inside them, not on some stone tablets. He said He would write His law on their hearts. Not in their hearts but on their hearts, because He wouldn't force Himself on anyone. Then He would be intimate and personal with them. God said He would forgive their wickedness and remember their sins no more. We don't have to have guilt, but how do we get rid of it? Yeshua tells us – through His blood. He said He would shed His blood for many for the remission of sins. Not for *all*? Didn't He shed His blood for all? Yes, but we have to receive it for ourselves. And many won't. The road to destruction is wide, and many will travel that road instead of the road provided by God. *Go in through the narrow gate; for the gate that leads to destruction is wide and the road broad, and many travel it* (Matthew 7:13).

Once more, consider the crimson worm in regard to Revelation 7:14. This worm secretes a crimson or scarlet gel during the birthing process that stains her body, her eggs, and the tree. The verse in Revelation says the tribulation saints *washed their robes and made them white with the blood of the Lamb.* There's only one way to be born again, and that's by being washed in the blood of the Lamb.

If you've ever stained something with blood, the two things you need to get it out are soap and salt. The Bible speaks of soap, the refiner's fuller soap, as a cleansing agent. *For he will be like a refiner's fire, like the soapmaker's lye* (Malachi 3:2). Salt is spoken of in Leviticus 2 as a preserving agent. *You are to season every grain offering of yours with salt – do not omit from your grain offering the salt of the covenant with your God, but offer salt with all your offerings* (Leviticus 2:13). The Bible says our sins are like *tola*; they are like the crimson worm. How can our blood-stained sins be washed with blood and yet become white? How does blood cleanse blood and make it white as snow? When the blood is so pure and so preserving it removes the stain of our blood guilt.

In the first chapter of Isaiah, we read, *"Come now," says* ADONAI, *"let's talk this over together. Even if your sins are like scarlet, they will be white as snow; even if they are red as crimson, they will be like wool"* (Isaiah 1:18). Do you hear the compassion in His appeal? He wasn't beating them up, but He was pleading with them to talk things over and use some logic to face the issue of sin. But by the same token, He wanted them to make a decision. His desire was for them to quit running and let Him fill that God-shaped hole for them. He said that even though their sins were as scarlet, like the gel stain from the crimson worm, by the blood of the Messiah they would be white as snow.

From the First Advent to the Second

After Yeshua had declared Himself to be a worm and cried to the Father to rescue Him, He called out:

Save me from the lion's mouth!
You have answered me from the wild bulls' horns.
I will proclaim your name to my kinsmen;
right there in the assembly I will praise you:
"You who fear ADONAI, praise him!
All descendants of Ya'akov [Jacob], glorify him!
All descendants of Isra'el, stand in awe of him!
For he has not despised or abhorred
the poverty of the poor;
he did not hide his face from him
but listened to his cry." (Psalm 22:21-24)

In these verses we're going from Golgotha to Olivet and from the first coming to the second. Was He saved from the lion's mouth? Yes, He was. He didn't stay in the tomb. He ascended, and He's coming back, and if we don't believe that, we have no hope.

If we use logic alone, this whole story makes little sense. Twelve guys give up everything to follow Him. Peter even gave up his family, and then they're confused when Yeshua is killed. They expected Him to take His throne. They wanted a messiah who was going to be their king, who would put down the Roman oppression and bring about the millennial kingdom – right then and there.

> He ascended, and He's coming back, and if we don't believe that, we have no hope.

However, if He did that at that time, we wouldn't have eternal life, and you would not be reading this book. Thankfully, God blinded their eyes, so more and more souls could inherit the kingdom of heaven.

The disciples were confused. They had thought the kingdom would be imminent, but Yeshua rose from the grave. His body had not been stolen. He rose. As we go back to Psalm 22:21-24, the Father answered Him, so right there in the assembly, Yeshua said He would praise the Father as the millennium began. He called on the sons of Jacob and the descendants of Israel to praise Him. The Father didn't hide His face from Him, but listened to His cry. Yeshua went from the cross to the crown right here in this psalm. We see that Yeshua is no longer speaking, but the Holy Spirit speaks as He says:

The poor will eat and be satisfied;
those who seek ADONAI will praise him;
Your hearts will enjoy life forever.
All the ends of the earth
will remember and turn to ADONAI;
all the clans of the nations
will worship in your presence.
For the kingdom belongs to ADONAI,
and he rules the nations.
All who prosper on the earth
will eat and worship;
all who go down to the dust
will kneel before him,
including him who can't keep himself alive.
(Psalm 22:26-29)

Look at what this time will be like: Poverty will be history, and the earth will be full of the Lord's praise. All the ends of the earth will remember and turn to ADONAI, as all the clans of the nations will worship. A world-wide revival will break

THE HEIGHT AND DEPTH OF THE MESSIAH'S LOVE

out, but this won't happen until Yeshua comes back. The next revival will hit Israel, and it will be the last and the greatest; then we'll see world-wide revival. Yeshua is getting ready to relight the fire, and every knee will bow to Yeshua. Anybody who is alive will bow.

The last two verses tell us:

> *A descendant will serve him;*
> *the next generation will be told of Adonai.*
> *They will come and proclaim*
> *his righteousness*
> *to a people yet unborn,*
> *that he is the one who did it.* (Psalm 22:30-31)

This means everybody will be worshipping the King. The next generation will be told about Him, and every time a child is born in the millennium, parents will tell him about Yeshua. They will come and praise Him, and parents won't have to worry any more. They will remember His last words on the cross: *It is finished.* He's the One who did it. The mission was accomplished, and nothing needs to be added to it.

> When we look at what an almighty God chose to do for us when He didn't have to, when we really believe this, our lives change.

Think about this incomprehensible fact – God became a man. He lowered Himself to be born as a baby. Then, God became a lamb, an animal who didn't open His mouth when He was led to the slaughter even though He was the Creator of the universe. Then the lamb became a worm, the lowest of all creatures, and the worm was crushed for you and me.

How much does God love us? When we look at what an

almighty God chose to do for us when He didn't have to, when we really believe this, our lives change. We change. Our focus turns to Him and living to please Him. It turns to eternity with Him.

Chapter 6

Living for God

The Greatest Commandment

U nderstanding the cross and salvation helps us understand how to live a life for God. Even the Torah teachers of Yeshua's time wanted to understand, but they didn't have the gospel of Mark, Revelation, or the New Testament. They were experts in the Law, but they sincerely wanted to understand how the Torah could be lived out in their lives. It was their foundation. That's why one of the Torah teachers approached Yeshua. He wasn't just an expert in the Torah but also in *halâkâh*, which is the way one should walk or live according to Torah teaching.

A particular Torah teacher in Mark 12 wasn't trying to be sarcastic, and he wasn't trying to trick Yeshua. Some of the others were, but not this one. He was serious, because he realized that this Man was a bona fide Rabbi with a fantastic connection with God, and His teachings were like none other. Mark recorded the encounter: *One of the Torah-teachers came up and heard them engaged in this discussion. Seeing that Yeshua answered them well, he asked him, "Which is the most important mitzvah* [commandment] *of them all?"* (Mark 12:28).

This Torah teacher was legitimate, and he really wanted to understand, because there were 613 commandments. He asked the question in all sincerity. "Which is the most important?" Yeshua didn't have to ponder or think about His answer. He knew immediately what was most important.

> *Yeshua answered, "The most important is, Hear, O Isra'el, the* LORD *our God, the* LORD *is one, and you are to love* ADONAI *your God with all your heart, with all your soul, with all your understanding and with all your strength."* (Mark 12:29)

Note that this gathering was a non-Gentile thing, as we see that only Jews were talking to Jews here. No Gentiles were involved. Even when Yeshua sent them out, He said, *"Don't go into the territory of the Goyim* [Gentiles], *and don't enter any town in Shomron* [Samaria], *but go rather to the lost sheep of the house of Isra'el"* (Matthew 10:5-6).

When Yeshua began to address the Torah teacher, He said, *Hear, O Israel.* That word *hear* is a word worth noting because it's the watchword, the rallying cry of Israel. He wanted them to hear, really hear. His desire was for them to listen and then obey what they heard. Any Jewish person knows what *shama* means – it's not just listening for the sake of listening. Many people listen but don't hear – not just in spiritual circles but in life. They do it all the time. Things go in one ear and out the other.

Many people listen but don't hear.

Yeshua was calling them to *shama* – to listen and obey. He talked to this Torah teacher and all the Jewish people and told them that the Lord is One. He said there's only one legitimate God – one God and nothing more. He also told them they were to love that one God with all their heart, mind, soul, and strength.

These words – *heart, soul, mind,* and *strength* – are in order of importance. As Yeshua prioritized these words, He deliberately put *heart* first. The Greek word is *kardia*, which means "the heart, inner life, intention." In the body, this organ is the center of the circulation of the blood. When our heart stops for a long period of time, we die, because it's the center of physical life. *Kardia* is also used to describe the center of spiritual life, the fountain or headwaters. It's the spring, the origination point for all our thoughts, our passions, and our purposes. We may think we know someone's heart, often we don't. We don't even know our own hearts at times. We don't know why we say some of the things we say, or why we do some of the things we do. The heart is the most important part of who we are because it's where all our decisions, thoughts, words, and deeds are born.

Next is the soul, the seat of feelings and emotions. This is the very place where we decide if something is funny or if it makes us happy, mad, or anxious. The soul is our decision maker – our will. Just having a soul, a decision maker, implies a choice. We get to choose whether we live for God or ourselves. We make choices every day, which indicate whether we chose God's way or our own way.

Moses encouraged the Israelites to choose when he said, *"Look! I am presenting you today with, on the one hand, life and good; and on the other, death and evil . . . I call on heaven and earth to witness against you today that I have presented you with life and death, the blessing and the curse. Therefore, choose life, so that you will live, you and your descendants"* (Deuteronomy 30:15, 19).

Later Joshua said, *"If it seems bad to you to serve ADONAI, then choose today whom you are going to serve! Will it be the gods your ancestors served beyond the River? or the gods of the Emori* [Amorites], *in whose land you are living? As for me and my household, we will serve ADONAI!"* (Joshua 24:15).

The mind is different from the heart and soul. The mind involves our way of thinking, and we each develop one way of thinking or another. Sometimes it's good, and sometimes it's not so good. We may ask each other, "What were you thinking?" In those cases, the person usually wasn't, but we've been given the ability to think and reason.

After the heart, soul, and mind comes the strength, and that's easy. Strength is our ability and our might. We're able to stand firm and persevere with our strength. So our heart dictates to our soul, and our soul dictates our understanding, and then we "walk it out." We don't just walk anything out without making a decision, but we shouldn't make a decision unless our heart is in it – good, bad, or indifferent. What we believe is crucial, for creed produces character, and not the other way around. We hear these important terms all the time but don't always understand. Sometimes we use them interchangeably, but they're different.

Another word we need to look at is *all* or *whole*, which comes from the Greek word *holos*, meaning "complete." The Hebrew word for *all* in Deuteronomy 6 means "everything." All is all. Complete. Everything. When God said He wants us to love Him with *all* our heart, it means *all* our heart. He doesn't want to share our heart. Likewise, when He said He wants all our mind, He wants it all. He wants all our thinking, all our reasoning, and all our decision-making. He wants our walk.

All? All our heart, soul, mind, and strength? Can we really do that? No, only Yeshua did that, but we can work toward that end. We can grow in the process of sanctification, giving God more of our heart, more of our soul, more of ourselves. Or, should we just admit that we can't do it, give up, and not even try? That would be ludicrous. God wants us to walk with Him closer and closer, day after day.

> God wants us to walk with Him closer and closer, day after day.

The Wizard of Oz

The 1939 edition of L. Frank Baum's book *The Wizard of Oz* seems to have some allegorical value here. Many godly people have used this story to portray biblical concepts. Atheists have used it, and the working class has used it to show parallels. Just think for a moment. We see the Tin Man who was looking for a heart; Dorothy was soulish, very emotional about going home; the Scarecrow was looking for a brain, and the Cowardly Lion wanted courage or strength. So all together they were searching for heart, soul, mind, and strength.

The Tin Man sang his song: "I'd be tender, I'd be gentle and awful sentimental, regarding love and art. I'd be friends with the sparrows and the boy who shoots the arrows, if I only had a heart."

We relate the Scarecrow to the brain and the mind. He had a memorable conversation with Dorothy, which went like this:

Dorothy: "How can you talk if you haven't got a brain?"

Scarecrow: "I don't know. But some people without brains do an awful lot of talking, don't they?"

Then the Cowardly Lion was looking for courage and strength. When faced with the need to save Dorothy, he said, "All right, I'll go in there for Dorothy. Wicked Witch or no Wicked Witch, guards or no guards. I'll tear them apart. I may not come out alive, but I'm going in there. There's only one thing I want you fellows to do."

The Scarecrow asked, "What's that?"

Cowardly Lion responded, "Talk me out of it."

And last, of course, Dorothy related to the soul. She wanted to go home, but didn't know how to get there. However, she had the answer all along – the ruby-red slippers. Sadly, many of us don't know what we've got until it's gone; only then, like the Prodigal Son do we realize, "There's no place like home."

The irony of the whole thing is that the Tin Man showed the most heart of all of them. He was the only one who teared up when they fell asleep right before getting to the Emerald City. He wept inconsolably. He was truly the one with the most heart. And the Scarecrow was actually the brains of the whole operation, because he devised the plan on how to get into the witch's castle to rescue Dorothy. Then the Cowardly Lion showed the most courage when he stormed the castle, but it was little Miss Dorothy who had the ability all along to get back home, where she truly wanted to be.

We can use *The Wizard of Oz* to portray each point of the greatest commandment. *And you are to love ADONAI your God with all your heart, with all your soul, with all your understanding and with all your strength* (Mark 12:30). Our Father has given us the means to accomplish this. He didn't leave us to work it out on our own, but He, the *Father of our Lord Yeshua the Messiah, who in the Messiah has blessed us with every spiritual blessing in heaven* (Ephesians 1:3). Also, 2 Peter 1:3 tells us *God's power has given us everything we need for life and godliness, through our knowing the One who called us to his own glory and goodness.* God asks us to love Him completely, but He provides the blessings and power necessary to do that.

When they got to the Emerald City, the wizard never gave them what they were looking for, because they had it all along. Therefore, some will say the film is about self-awareness, and we need to believe in ourselves to become whatever we imagine we want to be. Now, I am not a big fan of this kind of self-awareness because some things just aren't going to be. But I am a fan of the self-awareness that leads me to the realization that I can be heartless even though I have a heart. I can be mindless even if I have a pretty good brain. And, I can be way too focused on the external.

> God asks us to love Him completely, but He provides the blessings and power necessary to do that.

Our New Heart

Therefore, I believe we need to be made new and renewed on a regular basis. Initially, we need a makeover, not an Emerald City makeover but a heavenly city makeover that only happens through the rebirth. Nicodemus was the head teacher of the teachers, and he came to see Yeshua. He acknowledged that he knew Yeshua came from God because only a man from God could do those miracles. Yeshua got right to the point. He said, *"Yes, indeed . . . I tell you that unless a person is born again from above, he cannot see the Kingdom of God"* (John 3:3). Nicodemus questioned Him about returning to his mother's womb, but Yeshua told him he would not see heaven unless he was born again, explaining that what was born of water is water, but he needed to be born of the Spirit.

We need a new heart, because our inner heart has to be connected to God's heart. That's what initially happens when we repent and receive Yeshua for the forgiveness of our sins. When we receive Him as our innocent victim, as the only way to turn the redness of our sin to snow white, we receive the Holy Spirit, and our heart becomes connected to God's heart. This doesn't mean His heart will control us. We still make our own decisions, but we will hear from God. We will hear when He tells us no, go, or whatever He might say.

God spoke through Ezekiel saying, *I will give you a new heart and put a new spirit inside you; I will take the stony heart out of your flesh and give you a heart of flesh* (Ezekiel 36:26). Look at that word *new* – in the Hebrew it's *chadash*, meaning a fresh new thing, not something stale or that's been around. It's going to be new, not just restored. New, because now our heart is connected to God's heart, and they are beating together. We're able to hear God's heart on our heart, and the things that break God's heart will break our heart. The things that make God happy will make us happy. The things He detests, we should detest, and the things He couldn't care less about, we shouldn't care about.

Then, we'll not just get a new heart, we'll get a new mind. *"For this is the covenant which I will make with the house of Isra'el after those days," says* ADONAI: *"I will put my Torah in their minds and write it on their hearts; I will be their God, and they will be my people"* (Hebrews 8:10). It's not enough to get a new heart. We need a new mind also. In First Corinthians, Paul writes, *For who has known the mind of* ADONAI? *Who will counsel him? But we have the mind of the Messiah!* (1 Corinthians 2:16). Where did he get that? It comes straight out of Isaiah, and Isaiah didn't even come up with that – God did. This is a rhetorical question, who knows the mind of the Lord? No one.

But now, through the Holy Spirit, we can possess the mind of Messiah.. It's a new mind. In the Greek, the word for "new" is *kainos*. It's unprecedented, something brand-spanking new or unheard of – it's new. A new heart does new stuff, and a new mind has a whole new way of thinking.

If there's nothing new in our lives, how can we say we have a new heart? If we still hate the people we used to hate, what's new? Is something wrong on the divine side or the human side? We know it's a human issue. Our heart is connected and starts to dictate, but it can't force the words written on our heart. Even though we sometimes beat people up with the Bible, God never beats us up. He writes it on our heart, not in our heart. It's up to us to keep our heart soft. We have to break up the fallow ground – that's our heart. We have a hard heart, and God isn't going to break it up for us. It's up to us to humble ourselves, so the Word can get in, and as it's watered by the Holy Spirit, it germinates and bears fruit for His kingdom.

> A new heart does new stuff, and a new mind has a whole new way of thinking.

A word of advice here: We can't listen to ourselves. We need to talk to ourselves, but not listen, because we'll deceive ourselves. When we talk to ourselves, we dictate. All over the Psalms, David said, "I *will* praise the Lord." He commanded his heart to tell his mind to dictate to his soul, and then he walked it out. That was evidence of a new heart and new mind. But we still need new strength.

When a storm arose in Matthew 8, Yeshua said to them, *"Why are you afraid? So little trust you have!"* (Matthew 8:26).

He was telling them to have courage, to have strength. I grew up in a tough neighborhood, and I had to be tough. I had to be prepared to defend myself at school, even if I just went to the bathroom. I never knew what might be waiting for me, so I needed courage. Yeshua wasn't making fun of them. The Bible tells us over a hundred times not to be afraid, but we all still get scared at times.

Courage isn't the absence of fear. It's moving ahead in spite of the fear, because we'll never get rid of all our fears. If there was no fear, why would we need to be courageous? A quote that is often attributed to John Wayne says, "Courage is being scared to death but saddling up anyway." Hebrews 10:35 says, *So don't throw away that courage of yours, which carries with it such a great reward.* The writer was speaking to Jewish believers who were incredibly persecuted and told them not to throw their courage away. This means that they were operating courageously; they were afraid, but they were pressing forward. He told them courage and steadfastness carried a great reward, even more than just being saved.

> Courage isn't the absence of fear. It's moving ahead in spite of the fear

I remember one time at the ocean when I had to save a little child. The seven-foot waves were treacherous and threw us up and down. They washed over us, and I was taking in water and gasping for air. I felt so close to death that I knew it was going to be me or the child. I was drowning and didn't know what to do, but my instincts made me want to throw the child and save myself. I was so frantic. Finally, I felt something like a hand push me from behind – it pushed me up and over the swell, and I was able to get to the shore.. I was so out of breath that I laid there for twenty or thirty minutes before I reached an equilibrium again. The waves had been so treacherous and scary I had wanted to give up, but by the grace of God, I made it. That's how we feel sometimes when we want to say, "Enough already! Where are you, God?"

Like the cry of David in the Psalms, "How long? How long?" The Bible tells us to stand firm; when all else fails, stand firm, so that by having done what God wills, we may receive what He's promised. *So take up every piece of war equipment God provides; so that when the evil day comes, you will be able to resist; and when the battle is won, you will still be standing* (Ephesians 6:13).

The new heart, new soul, new mind, and new strength we've got are not from thin air. They are from the Lord. They're not from the ruby-red slippers, but they're from the ruby-red blood of the Messiah. *You should be aware that the ransom paid to free you from the worthless way of life which your fathers passed on to you did not consist of anything perishable like silver or gold* (1 Peter 1:18). This new heart and new mind is made powerful and possible through the blood of Yeshua. Peter said we should be aware that a ransom was paid because we had been kidnapped, hoodwinked, and robbed of our excellence. But in the midst of all of that, we robbed God of His worship. Peter told us that a ransom was paid to free us from our worthless way of life, but the ransom wasn't any treasure of silver, gold, or precious gems. It was the costly, bloody, sacrificial death of the Messiah, a Lamb without spot or defect.

Living with Our New Heart

Consider the apostle Paul, the Jews' Jew. He was very proud of his Jewish heritage, training, and aptitude, but when he met the Messiah, he felt crushed. He felt like he didn't deserve to live and no longer cared about his accolades. In fact, he couldn't have cared less. He considered all his accomplishments as dung. He stated, *"Not only that, but I consider everything a disadvantage in comparison with the supreme value of knowing the Messiah Yeshua as my Lord. It was because of him that I gave up everything and regard it all as garbage, in order to gain the Messiah"* (Philippians 3:8). All he knew was the Messiah and Him crucified, and he shared it and shared it. *For I had decided that while I was with you I would forget everything except Yeshua the Messiah, and even him only as someone who had been executed on a stake as a criminal* (1 Corinthians 2:2). Oh happy day, the day we get saved; but oh what a happier day when we go to be with Him. We beg God not to let us die, but Paul said to die is gain. *For to me, life is the Messiah, and death is gain* (Philippians 1:21). Do we really believe that? Is it true? Is the happiest day the day when Yeshua comes back? Wouldn't it be nice to just click our heels three times and go home? But we're not home yet.

We have no permanent city here; on the contrary, we seek the one to come (Hebrews 13:14). Knowing this, we still hang on to our earthly homes. Sometimes we even worship our homes, but our houses are not our homes. We are out of place. The first lines of a Jim Reeves' gospel song say it well: "This world is not my home, I'm just a passin' through." As believers, we don't fit in anymore; we just don't belong.

So, we're looking for something, and it's not coming over the rainbow – it's coming down from heaven. *Then I saw a new heaven and a new earth, for the old heaven and the old earth had passed away, and the sea was no longer there. Also I saw the holy city, New Yerushalayim [Jerusalem], coming down out of heaven from God, prepared like a bride beautifully dressed for her husband* (Revelation 21:1-2). Not only do we get a new heart, a new mind, and new courage, but we also get a brand-new home. A new heaven and a new earth are coming from God, but by the time we see this happen, the millennium will be over, and we will have sat under the teachings of Yeshua for a thousand years. We will have been blessed, because we will have experienced the first resurrection and been taught by the King.

I've never found the yellow brick road, but I'm looking forward to the streets of gold described in Revelation 21:21. *The twelve gates were twelve pearls, with each gate made of a single pearl. The city's main street was pure gold, transparent as glass.* This is the glory of God. We're not talking about justification here, and we're not talking about sanctification either. They are over – done. We're looking at glorifica-

> Eternal life is in a class of its own – it's truly a gift in every sense of the word.

tion, and it's pure. We can't fathom what it's going to look like. We've never experienced a pure heart, pure thinking, and pure strength. But we will.

Every accolade in life is earned. People get Congressional Medals of Honor, Pulitzers, championship titles, and gold medals. People are even listed with the Guinness World Records. But eternal life is in a class of its own – it's truly a gift in every sense of the word with no real strings attached. When you think about it, doesn't it just make you fall on your knees with your face to the ground and ask the Lord how you got here? Isaiah told us, *But those who die in the LORD will live; their bodies will rise again! Those who sleep in the earth will rise up and sing for joy!* (Isaiah 26:19 NLT). This isn't just a New Testament concept. It's a God concept. What Daniel said of this time is true. *Many of those whose bodies lie dead and buried will rise up, some to everlasting life and some to shame and everlasting disgrace* (Daniel 12:2 NLT).

There are only two choices. For every single solitary aspect of God's kingdom and spirituality, there are two choices, not three or four or five. Just one or the other. More importantly, in the gospel of John, Yeshua said, *"Don't be surprised at this; because the time is coming when all who are in the grave will hear his voice and come out – those who have done good to a resurrection of life, and those who have done evil to a resurrection of judgment"* (John 5:28-29). Grace people often struggle with these verses, particularly if we read

> For every single solitary aspect of God's kingdom and spirituality, there are two choices, not three or four or five. Just one or the other.

them out of context or we aren't grounded in all the Scriptures. He's not saying we will rise to eternal life if we do good stuff. He's not even saying the good stuff of obedience is the root of our salvation. He's saying it's the fruit of our salvation; that's how we know we're saved. If our conscience in our heart isn't aligned with God, and we just casually walk by a homeless person without it affecting us, something's wrong. If pictures on television of starving children cause us to want to change the channel because we don't want to feel bad, something's wrong. Something is radically wrong.

I read an article some time ago that referred to John 5:28-29. A woman in London had asked some workmen to seal up her tomb when she died. She was an enemy of the Christian faith and was attempting to prove a point that she didn't intend to come forth to a resurrection of life or of damnation. The workmen sealed up the tomb with steel-reinforced concrete. Then they engraved the words "dead forever" on the tomb. "No way is this body going to come out of this grave," agreed the workmen as they surveyed the tomb. Below the words was inscribed the quote: "Marvel not at this for the hour is never coming when the person in this grave will hear His voice or any other voice. She will never come forth either to a resurrection of life or resurrection of damnation."

Everybody's entitled to their opinion. Nobody can stop them from putting it on their tomb, but notice the antagonism. One year after they put her in the tomb, a tiny crack in the concrete appeared, caused by a tiny shoot from an oak tree that was next to it. Within a few years, the grave was literally split wide open by the trunk of the tree that had grown from that insignificant plant. The power of that life burst the bands of steel in the concrete to declare to the woman, "It is futile." She opted for a choice that wasn't hers. What happens after our resurrection is optional, but our resurrection isn't. Every single soul will be resurrected.

A good friend of mine recently passed away. It was totally unexpected. He and his wife had just returned from a vacation and were in the process of expanding their ministry when he got pneumonia, had a heart attack, and died.

He was born in 1948 and left us in 2016, so his headstone would read 1948-2016. My friend didn't have a choice in his birth; that decision was made for him. And although he took great care of himself, his death was also a decision that was out of his hands. We may prolong our days on earth, but statistically speaking, one out of one of us still dies. But what about that little dash between our birth date and our death date? That little dash encompasses *all* our decision-making. We decide everything from what we'll eat, to where we live, and everything in between. What most people don't realize is that there's a second dash. It's the dash that represents eternity, and it comes after our death date. So in reality, my friend's headstone should read 1948-2016-. Everyone has the second dash, but truth be told, the decisions made during the first dash dictate our final destination.

If you haven't made God and Yeshua your choice during that little dash, I wholeheartedly suggest that you do that now. Let Him be the innocent victim, because either you're going to accept His blood, or you'll have to be responsible for it.

Ask Him for a heart like His. Make the choice that leads to eternal life; then live each day for God.

Yeshua said He didn't come to condemn the world but to save it. God doesn't send anybody away from heaven. It's our choice. Meet with God, repent, and tell Him you're sorry. Ask Him for a heart like His. Make the choice that leads to eternal life; then live each day for God. Walk in this world with eternity in view, hand in hand with your loving Father.

Concluding Comments

This is the revelation which God gave to Yeshua the Messiah, so that he could show his servants what must happen very soon. He communicated it by sending his angel to his servant Yochanan [John], who bore witness to the Word of God and to the testimony of Yeshua the Messiah, as much as he saw. Blessed are the reader and hearers of the words of this prophecy, provided they obey the things written in it! For the time is near!

From: Yochanan
To: The seven Messianic communities in the prov-
ince of Asia:

Grace and shalom [peace] *to you from the One who*
is, who was and who is coming.
(Revelation 1:1-4)

This beginning of Revelation, the last book of the Bible, takes us back to the tripartite aspect of God – the One who was, who is, and who is to come. Here is the first key to experiencing a life for God, for how can we even begin to understand, appreciate, and love Him without knowing what He did in the past for us, how He's caring for and directing us now, and that He promises to return in glory?

As detailed earlier, Psalm 22 describes the mission of the God who was. David referenced the earthly birth of Yeshua, but gives great detail of the crucifixion and separation from His Father. We can see the obedience and suffering of Yeshua who willingly gave His life as the Passover Lamb. He explained this in John:

> *"I am the good shepherd. The good shepherd lays*
> *down his life for the sheep . . . I am the good shep-*
> *herd; I know my own, and my own know me – just*
> *as the Father knows me, and I know the Father – and*
> *I lay down my life on behalf of the sheep . . . This is*
> *why the Father loves me: because I lay down my life*
> *– in order to take it up again! No one takes it away*
> *from me; on the contrary, I lay it down of my own*
> *free will. I have the power to lay it down, and I have*

*the power to take it up again. This is what my Father
commanded me to do.* (John 10:11, 14-15, 17-18)

Five times Yeshua mentioned laying down His own life, and
then He referenced His obedience to His Father. He is the Good
Shepherd who also becomes our Passover Lamb. He is the God
who was. But after we see the suffering of Yeshua in this psalm,
David ends with hope. He speaks of the kingdom of Adonai
and eating and worshipping on the earth with Him.

Psalm 23 is the picture of the Great Shepherd. It begins,
ADONAI is my shepherd; I lack nothing. Hebrews 13:20-21 sheds
more light on this Shepherd:

> *The God of shalom brought up from the dead the
> great Shepherd of the sheep, our Lord Yeshua, by the
> blood of an eternal covenant. May that God equip
> you with every good thing you need to do his will;
> and may he do in us whatever pleases him, through
> Yeshua the Messiah. To him be the glory forever and
> ever. Amen.*

This is the resurrected Shepherd who indwells us, walks with us
in this life, and empowers us to carry on a life for God. This is
the role of the Holy Spirit. Where Psalm 22 depicted Passover,
Psalm 23 depicts Shavuot or Pentecost. This psalm once again
ends with a vision of the future hope – sitting at the table and
living in the house of Adonai.

Then Psalm 24 gives us the picture of the Chief Shepherd,
the God who will come again. This psalm is representative of
Sukkot, the Feast of Tabernacles, when God will tabernacle or

live among men. The whole psalm is praise to Adonai when He rules on earth. It is truly a song of praise:

> Lift up your heads, you gates!
> Lift them up, everlasting doors,
> so that the glorious king can enter!
> Who is he, this glorious king?
>
> *Adonai, strong and mighty,*
> *Adonai, mighty in battle.*
>
> *Lift up your heads, you gates!*
> *Lift them up, everlasting doors,*
> *so that the glorious king can enter!*
> *Who is he, this glorious king!*
> *Adonai-Tzva'ot –*
> *he is the glorious king.* (Psalm 24:7-10)

Peter also referred to this Chief Shepherd as he wrote to the Jews who were being persecuted throughout Asia Minor. He told them, "*Then, when the Chief Shepherd appears, you will receive glory as your unfading crown*" (1 Peter 5:4). Surely, he recognized the Chief Shepherd as the God who would return.

So we see Psalms 22, 23, and 24 representing the God who was, the God who is, and the God who will come again. We see the Good Shepherd, the Great Shepherd, and the Chief Shepherd in these psalms, as we see the three feasts – Passover, Pentecost, and the Feast of Tabernacles. In addition to that, we see justification by the God who was, sanctification by the God who is, and glorification by the God who will come again.

When we look at the whole picture, it allows us to come

back to the original questions, "What shall I do to gain eternal life? How can I maintain a life for God?" Yeshua told them, *You are to love ADONAI your God with all your heart, with all your soul, with all your strength and with all your understanding.* In doing that, we will live for eternity, because all our doings will be determined by our desire to be pleasing to the Father. We will be living for God.

Again, if you haven't made God and Yeshua your choice within the little dash between your birth and your final day, I wholeheartedly suggest that you do that now. Let Him be the victim, because either you're going to accept His blood, or you'll have to pay for it.

God doesn't send anybody away from heaven. It's our choice. Meet with God, repent, and tell Him you're sorry. Ask Him for a heart like His. Make the choice that leads to eternal life. Then live each day for God. Walk in this world with eternity in view, hand in hand with your loving Father.

> *"Pay attention!" [says Yeshua,] "I am coming soon, and my rewards are with me to give to each person according to what he has done. I am the Alpha and the Omega, the First and the Last, the Beginning and the End."*
> (Revelation 22:12-13)

Come, Lord Yeshua, Come!

Meet the Author

Rabbi Greg Hershberg was born in New York City and raised in Orthodox Judaism. He graduated Pace University, Magna Cum Laude and later owned and operated an executive search firm in New York City, specializing in banking and finance. In 1989, he married Bernadette and while on his honeymoon in Israel had a visitation from the Lord that turned his heart to serving God.

In 1992, Rabbi Greg became involved in the Messianic Jewish Movement and was ordained through the International Association of Messianic Congregations and Synagogues (IAMCS). He became the leader of Beth Judah Messianic Congregation. In 2002, the Lord moved Rabbi Greg and his family to Macon, Georgia, to lead Congregation Beth Yeshua.

The ministry went global in 2010 and Congregation Beth Yeshua became Beth Yeshua International (BYI). What was a local storefront congregation became an international ministry/training center in Macon, Georgia, with congregations and schools in India, Kenya, Australia, Germany, Israel, and across America. In addition, Rabbi Greg's messages are live-streamed throughout the world.

Rabbi Greg currently resides in Macon, Georgia, with his wife, Bernadette, and their four children. More about Rabbi Greg can be found in his autobiography, *From The Projects To The Palace*.

To learn more about Rabbi Greg Hershberg:

www.getzel.org

Updated Classics by

Often disguised as something that would help him, evil accompanies Christian on his journey to the Celestial City. As you walk with him, you'll begin to identify today's many religious pitfalls. These are presented by men such as Pliable, who turns back at the Slough of Despond; and Ignorance, who believes he's a true follower of Christ when he's really only trusting in himself. Each character represented in this allegory is intentionally and profoundly accurate in its depiction of what we see all around us, and unfortunately, what we too often see in ourselves. But while Christian is injured and nearly killed, he eventually prevails to the end. So can you.

The best part of this book is the Bible verses added to the text. The original *Pilgrim's Progress* listed the Bible verse references, but the verses themselves are so impactful when tied to the scenes in this allegory, that they are now included within the text of this book. The text is tweaked just enough to make it readable today, for the young and the old. Youngsters in particular will be drawn to the original illustrations included in this wonderful classic.

Available where books are sold.

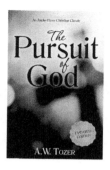

To have found God and still to pursue Him is a paradox of love, scorned indeed by the too-easily-satisfied religious person, but justified in happy experience by the children of the burning heart. Saint Bernard of Clairvaux stated this holy paradox in a musical four-line poem that will be instantly understood by every worshipping soul:

> *We taste Thee, O Thou Living Bread,*
> *And long to feast upon Thee still:*
> *We drink of Thee, the Fountainhead*
> *And thirst our souls from Thee to fill.*

Come near to the holy men and women of the past and you will soon feel the heat of their desire after God. Let A. W. Tozer's pursuit of God spur you also into a genuine hunger and thirst to truly know God.

Available where books are sold.

Made in United States
North Haven, CT
01 June 2023

37235338R00085